BLOOD BROTHERS

JOHN GRANT

BLOOD BROTHERS

*The division and decline of
Britain's trade unions*

Weidenfeld & Nicolson
London

First published in Great Britain in 1992 by
George Weidenfeld and Nicolson Limited
91 Clapham High Street, London SW4 7TA

British Library Cataloguing-in-Publication Data is
available on request.

ISBN 0 297 81238 6

Typeset by Deltatype Ltd, Ellesmere Port
Printed and bound in Great Britain by
Butler & Tanner Ltd
Frome and London

Contents

Illustrations

Abbreviations

ACAS	Advisory, Conciliation and Arbitration Service
AEU	Amalgamated Engineering Union
AUEW	Amalgamated Union of Engineering Workers
ASLEF	Association of Locomotive Engineers and Firemen
ASTMS	Association of Supervisory, Technical and Managerial Staffs
BIFU	Banking, Insurance and Finance Union
CLV	Campaign for Labour Victory
CND	Campaign for Nuclear Disarmament
CPSA	Civil and Public Services Association
CSD	Civil Service Department
CIR	Commission for Industrial Relations
CIM	Commission for Industry and Manpower
CRE	Commission for Racial Equality
CBI	Confederation of British Industry
DEA	Department of Economic Affairs
DHSS	Department of Health and Social Security
EETPU	Electrical, Electronic, Telecommunication and Plumbing Union
ETU	Electrical Trades Union
FDA	First Division Association
GEC	General Electric Company
GMBATU	General, Municipal, Boilermakers and Allied Trades Union
GMWU	General and Municipal Workers' Union
HSC	Health and Safety Commission
IRSF	Inland Revenue Staff Federation
MSF	Manufacturing, Science and Finance
NALGO	National and Local Government Officers' Association
NEDC	National Economic Development Council (Neddy)

NGA	National Graphical Association
NIC	National Incomes Commission (Nicky)
NIRC	National Industrial Relations Court
NUJ	National Union of Journalists
NUM	National Union of Mineworkers
NUPE	National Union of Public Employees
NUR	National Union of Railwaymen
NUS	National Union of Seamen
ODA	Overseas Development Administration
ODM	Ministry of Overseas Development
PFA	Professional Footballers' Association
PIB	National Board for Prices and Incomes
SOGAT	Society of Graphical and Allied Trades
TUC	Trades Union Congress
TGWU	Transport and General Workers' Union
TSSA	Transport Salaried Staffs Association
UCATT	Union of Construction Allied Trades and Technicians
UDM	Union of Democratic Mineworkers
USDAW	Union of Shop, Distributive and Allied Workers

Foreword

Trade unions today appear, at best, as well-meaning but enfeebled and incompetent protectors of working people's interests and as a necessary but inefficient antidote to employer power. At worst, they present themselves as dictatorial, politically motivated troublemakers. But whatever the judgement, one thing is incontrovertible: they are an integral part of life's awkward squad.

It is therefore appropriate that I should have been so closely concerned with them for so long and should write this account of their deeds and misdeeds over the past three decades, for I am unashamedly part of that same awkward squad.

Bagehot claimed that the English are 'a deferential people'. Not all of us. I have trod, with few regrets, on the toes of a succession of distinguished establishment figures – royals, prime ministers and party leaders, with a trade union bigwig or two thrown in for good measure. All this in a somewhat unusual, even unique, working life in the media, politics and the unions.

One wise old newspaper friend once advised me: 'Never resign from anything. Always let them fire you.' He was right but it was not a creed I could follow. I quit the *Daily Express* in pique but, more by fluke than design, was invited back before my departure took effect. I offered my resignation to Prime Minister Harold Wilson rather than continue in a ministerial backwater and was generously switched by him to another post.

I risked the sack from ministerial office by refusing to vote for excessive royal pay rises when low-paid workers' wages were pegged, and told Labour's whips: 'I always vote Labour but I can't vouch for the Queen.' I opposed, from within, the Labour Government's plans to

xi

boost jobs by warship sales to the oppressive Argentinian regime. I deliberately broke ministerial rules of conduct on several occasions to campaign for the socially just incomes policy which, even now, I believe is vital to any non-Conservative economic policy.

Much earlier, I was briefly a Young Liberal, progressing there naturally from the Mickey Mouse Fan Club. I found the Young Liberals a fractious, self-seeking bunch, mostly aspiring to be big fish in a very small pond. I moved on, via the Fabian Society, to the Labour Party. I shall never regret that, though it eventually brought me to the most agonizing decision of all – my break with Labour after twenty-six years membership because of its seemingly irreversible leftwards slide. I admit that I left my political heart behind.

Life has never been dull. I have been the confidant of some of our best-known politicians and union leaders. I have rubbed shoulders with the rich and powerful, have been angered by the pomposity, authoritarianism and zealotry around in public life, have been sickened by the stench of the developing world's dire poverty and have marvelled at the selfless dedication of those who unceasingly fight to overcome that poverty. The qualities which I most admire are compassion and a sense of humour.

I was born on 16 October 1932, at Finsbury Park, North London, just over the borough boundary from the Islington constituency which I later represented in parliament for thirteen years.

I had no doubts about the job which I wanted. Journalism was my goal. Early in 1953 I started work as a reporter on the *Christchurch Times*, a small-circulation weekly on the South Coast.

Fleet Street was Mecca. All the old sweats advised me against being quick and slippery-footed. It was not advice which I wanted to hear. I had short spells on the bi-weekly *Wisbech Advertiser* and on the *Grimsby Evening Telegraph* and then, against all the conventions, made it fast to Grub Street, the Street of Shame, the Street of Adventure, the Street of Ink, the Street of Opportunity – the pseudonyms abounded.

I resorted to a gimmick to get there. I wrote to the *Daily Express*'s Arthur Christiansen, perhaps the greatest in the Fleet Street editors' roll of honour. My letter eulogized, in racy *Express*-style terms, a bright young talent which the paper couldn't afford to ignore. Immodestly, I meant me. *Express* news editor Morley Richards replied to say that Chris passed my letter to him – 'a most ingenious application'. I was hired.

On 10 October 1955, my dream became a reality. I began reporting from the most famous newspaper building in the world, the black glass-fronted 'Lubianka' which housed what was then Britain's biggest circulation daily, and deservedly so. I was aged twenty-two, and on three months trial at what seemed to me to be the handsome salary of eighteen guineas a week. I think that I was then Fleet Street's youngest reporter.

I was taken on as a working reporter, not one of the left-wing élite directly recruited by the *Express*'s mercurial, if malevolently right-wing proprietor, Lord Beaverbrook, whose capricious habit was to make selected socialists offers which they somehow couldn't refuse. The most illustrious of these was Michael Foot, whose close relationship with the virulently anti-socialist Beaverbrook was in strange contrast to Foot's much-trumpeted leftist purity.

I reported general news for the next five years. They were still great days on the *Express*. Money was no object. The paper swamped the big stories with its staff and to considerable effect. The *Express* was customarily out in front in the race for news, home and abroad. Saturation coverage was the order of the day.

Not long after I joined the right-wing *Daily Express*, contrary as ever, I joined the Labour Party, too. I equated Labour with 'social justice', a term which, however ill-defined, meant much to me and has virtually disappeared from our national vocabulary, including Labour's. I canvassed keenly for the party of 'social justice' at elections and went to meetings whenever my shift work pattern allowed.

Political activity was difficult because of my job, but I revived a moribund ward Labour Party and several times contested seats for the local council. It was safe Tory territory and I could show the Labour flag as a candidate who couldn't expect to win.

I became increasingly interested in politics and trade unionism. I applied for a second time to fill a vacancy as deputy to the *Express*'s chief industrial reporter, Trevor Evans, and was appointed. I was aged twenty-seven.

It was 1960 and the start of my intimacy with the trade unions. It heralded thirty years or so of involvement in the wider Labour movement, much of which is recorded in this book.

I present neither an autobiography nor an all-embracing industrial history of those times. My own treble role – as national newspaper journalist, as MP and minister and as national trade union official – is, to the best of my knowledge, unmatched. I chart most of the significant events as I experienced them and now recall them with the benefit of hindsight.

I deal primarily with what I have witnessed, can verify and can therefore properly interpret. That makes the Labour movement authentic subject matter. I am less well qualified to deal with the kind of corporate sector abuse which is the justifiable cause of far more public concern today than any union deficiencies. By this I mean such matters as the huge pay rises to directors, unlinked to any improvements in company fortunes, or the inadequate regulation of financial and business institutions that has allowed a succession of free market scandals to rival the inherent corruption of unrestrained state tyrannies.

The Conservative government claims that it is wrong to assume that the process of transforming trade unions and industrial relations is complete or that progress has been sufficient or is permanent. The further industrial relations legislation which it plans to introduce if it wins another general election is largely unnecessary but would be more convincing if accompanied by citizen-friendly measures for private-sector companies.

It is not only the unions that must change to meet the challenges of the next century if our children and their children are to prosper.

1

Endangered Species

Britain's trade union movement heads towards the year 2000 in a state of confusion, division and decline. The unions remain incapable of answering with any confidence or coherence the crucial question succinctly posed nearly thirty years ago by the then Trades Union Congress General Secretary, George Woodcock. He asked, reflectively: 'What are we here for?'

Instead of producing a practical and constructive response to this question, the unions have down the years exercised their negative power in a largely irresponsible way that has earned them public scorn and enmity. They first buttressed, then bludgeoned, Labour under Harold Wilson in the sixties. They were the biggest single factor in his 1970 general election defeat, and went on to bring down the Heath and Callaghan governments in 1974 and 1979 respectively. They learned little from their catalogue of errors, arrogance and recklessness.

The eighties brought harsh retribution. Mrs Thatcher confronted and conquered them. Hers was a populist cause, and she imposed stringent legal restraints which found favour with the electorate, including very many trade unionists. She ignored and humiliated the TUC, the unions' central command, which was for so long an ex-officio wing of the political establishment.

Mrs Thatcher has departed the scene, but the shrivelled and chastened unions continue to drift, having lost membership, money and muscle. An impotent TUC is still sidelined by the Tories. Even Labour, conscious of the risk of a recurrent political backlash from a fulsome renewal of the old overtly incestuous relationship, is more cautious of its natural ally than ever before.

The TUC and its affiliated unions are feebly led. In 1988 the

1

movement was fractured by the TUC's foolhardy expulsion of the EETPU, the electricians' union. Non-unionism spreads, along with calculated derecognition of unions by employers. Altogether, it is a deeply depressing scenario for those who recognize that although the unions habitually parade their vices, they have virtues which mostly go unrecorded.

The British trade union movement is a muddled mixture of thoughtlessness and compassion, envy and concern, deceit and fidelity. Unions are usually more misguided than malevolent. They tend to be reactionary and conservative, rather than radical. Their disorderly and ill-defined economic and social ambitions are based on good intent – broadly to improve the wellbeing of their members, but their actions frequently undermine that intent to the detriment of everyone, including the members they purport to serve. Small wonder that they receive such acrid criticism.

The TUC annual conference traditionally ends with the delegates holding hands and singing Auld Lang Syne in a display of togetherness – a display which impresses only the gullible. Unity is strength, but it is disunity which predominates today, as the unions slither downwards in a seemingly unstoppable slide. Trade unionists should be blood brothers but they have given the phrase new meaning. Much of the blood which they have needlessly spilled in recent times has been that of other trade unionists, even within their own organizations. Healthy diversity within and between unions is one thing, but naked hatred and vicious rivalry is another. Any example of this, well publicized, can undo months of painstaking effort to polish an already badly tarnished union image and is a surefire disincentive to any potential recruit.

The unions are an endangered species, akin to prehistoric dinosaurs. Their sorry condition is largely of their own making. They are their own worst enemies whatever claim the Conservative Party or the Institute of Directors may lay to that title. It is essential to their survival that membership is seen to be a worthwhile investment for those whom they seek to represent. True, unemployment has hit their numbers hard. But more and more of those in work take a look at the unions and vote with their feet.

The outstanding issue for the politicians is no longer union power. Margaret Thatcher's political will and legislative clout saw to that. Prime Minister Major is untroubled by 'the union question' which preoccupied his predecessors. Strikes are dramatically down, though once again unemployment is as much a reason for that as is legislation and union emasculation.

Now, robbed of their virility, it is more vital than ever for the unions to respond constructively to Woodcock's question. The TUC cannot be more than the sum of its parts. Today though, it is less meaningful than at any time since thirty-four delegates, representing some 118,000 trade union members, attended the first Congress in the Mechanics' Institute, Manchester, in 1868. That tiny debating assembly grew into a national representative body which went on to play a positive part in securing radical changes in British society and in the structure of our industry.

The TUC used to be the authentic voice of working people. Governments of various colours recognized its intrinsic contribution to the conduct of the nation's affairs. So, reluctantly, did the employers. There was a continuing industrial dialogue and a substantial consensus, something still regarded as the norm in most of Europe, where governments, unions and employers operate as 'social partners'.

Ernest Bevin, Churchill's Minister of Labour during the Second World War, was the architect and first General Secretary of the biggest union, the Transport and General Workers' (TGWU). Bevin, the workers' mandarin, became Foreign Secretary in Attlee's post-war Labour administration. He was the embodiment of the trade union statesman who, more than anyone, ensured the unions' unchallengeable place at the nation's top table as the Fifth Estate of the Realm.

The TUC's horny-handed heavyweights in the forties and fifties – Arthur Deakin, Tom Williamson, Will Lawther – led the big manual unions. No government minister brushed them irreverently aside. Theirs was an authoritarian right-wing rule, and they rarely failed to carry their members with them.

Cousins and Woodcock

Frank Cousins unexpectedly captured power in the TGWU in 1956 and, with remarkable rapidity, pulled the entire trade union movement leftwards. He imposed his own brand of autocracy on the TGWU, rampaged through the TUC and harangued governments, Tory and Labour alike. His impact on the Labour Party was similarly dramatic. He may have been the bully with the big block vote but Cousins, often in close alliance with Woodcock, saw to it that the TUC was respectfully, even fearfully, listened to.

The two were formidable personalities. Woodcock, a philosophical, pensive, working-class intellectual with a first-class Oxford degree, was openly intolerant of the bulk of the TUC General Council, the sometimes less than gifted bunch of union leaders who are charged with policy-making between the annual TUC conferences. He found in the ex-lorry driver Cousins, a man with whom he could deal on roughly equal terms. What Cousins lacked in subtlety and intellect he made up for with a mixture of instinctive political nous and single-minded determination – a determination that could spill over into self-righteousness and pigheaded irrationality.

Two such dominant figures were sure to fall out. The inevitable breach came over Labour's wage restraint policies. Woodcock understood the economic damage inherent in an unbridled scramble for bigger pay packets. Cousins – other than during an unhappy and uncomfortable spell in the Labour Cabinet – trumpeted his demand for unrestricted free collective bargaining throughout Harold Wilson's 1964–70 premiership.

Unions regnant

Despite the tension between the Labour government and the unions during this period, every royal commission, every quango, had its TUC-nominated appointee. Ministers hobnobbed constantly with the TUC top brass and interfered with the TUC pecking order at their peril. No. 10 Downing Street was a second home to Woodcock and the trade union select. Yet the government got a poor rate of return for its investment. Woodcock accepted the hard facts of economic life, but too few of his TUC colleagues were willing or able to endorse his views, and agreement with Wilson over pay foundered.

By the time Labour capitulated to the unions over Wilson's trade union reform package, 'In Place of Strife', Woodcock, careworn and unfulfilled, had been replaced as TUC General Secretary by his deputy, Vic Feather, a shrewd fixer, as jocularly folksy as Woodcock was morose. It was time for Cousins too, to go. His successor, Jack Jones, forceful and intense, maintained the left-wing grip on the TGWU. Bill Carron, longtime right-wing president of the engineers' union, retired, and left-winger Hugh Scanlon hijacked what was then the second biggest union. Jones and Scanlon, the so-called 'terrible twins', took the TUC in tow.

The débâcle over 'In Place of Strife' demonstrated union power at its most relentless. Wilson accused his own Cabinet of cowardice but he

4

and his Employment Minister, Barbara Castle, were forced to back down. The block votes of the recalcitrant unions controlled the Labour Party conference. Their influence over their sponsored MPs was circuitous but exacting. Wilson could not hold the parliamentary line. 'Even the best regulated family needs a slipper', Wilson told a TUC delegation at Downing Street. 'You don't keep it on the mantelpiece though', retorted Feather. The legislative slipper was tossed into the political dustbin. The last word on the matter came from an electorate deeply disenchanted by the Labour Cabinet's ill-disguised surrender. The 'union question' was decisive in Labour's 1970 downfall.

The incoming Conservative government, under Edward Heath, sought to pick up where Labour left off. Heath introduced his own industrial relations reform and tried to produce an acceptable pay policy, but the unions would have none of it. They had not thwarted Labour simply to have a Tory version thrust upon them. They marched against Heath's trade union legislation, chanting 'Kill the Bill'. There was strike after strike over pay, and one state of emergency followed another.

The National Union of Mineworkers, led by a wily little Lancastrian, Joe Gormley, finally scuppered any deal on wages. Heath rashly went to the country in 1974 on a 'who governs?' ticket. He was convinced that the public would give the overbearing unions their comeuppance. Instead, the strike-battered electorate put more of the blame on him, and Labour was returned to office, albeit with a minuscule parliamentary majority.

Meanwhile, the ebullient Feather had been superseded at the TUC by his second-in-command, Len Murray, civil, conscientious, caring and ill at ease in advancing the more excessive demands of the unions. It was Jones now who occupied the TUC driving seat and, eschewing his more left-wing instincts, pressed for a series of legislative changes that would bring the unions back to a position of power and influence in the country's economic and social development. The Social Contract, a government–union bargain on wage restraint and other related issues, was in vogue. Jones was its procreator.

The unions were nurtured by Wilson and then by his Downing Street successor, James Callaghan. TUC-affiliated membership soared from nine to twelve million. Britain had the biggest trade union movement per head of working population of all the Western industrialized nations. But despite their ebullience, the unions, shortsighted and impatient for more jam today, grew tired of responding to Labour's

5

economic difficulties. The 1978–9 Winter of Discontent found the Labour government and the unions locked into a fatal conflict, once more over wage restraint. Retirement had claimed both Jones and Scanlon, and Murray was helpless to rescue a situation that spiralled out of control.

Thatcherism triumphant: union reform

The ensuing 1979 general election was Mrs Thatcher's triumph. She swept home on a platform that blazoned trade union reform as its centrepiece, and from then on, it was downhill all the way for the unions. One piece of Conservative legislation followed and complemented another, until the unions found themselves unable to function without a hip-pocket lawyer. What Employment Ministers Jim Prior and Norman Tebbit began, their lengthy list of ministerial successors have enthusiastically maintained.

Prior did Thatcher's bidding. His was the first of the six legislative tracts which have steadily withered away union sinew. However, Prior wielded the big stick with diffidence, and never with the vigour to satisfy Margaret Thatcher. Not so Tebbit. The lugubrious son of a pawn-broker, Tory by conviction, not birth, Tebbit treated the unions with gleeful thespian menace. Privately amenable, Tebbit contemptuously taunted the bemused TUC, correctly calculating that an outraged over-reaction would provide him with political kudos from a public that was heartily sick of union bluster and fulmination.

Some Conservative changes were, indeed, long overdue. There was, after all, no convincing argument against pre-strike ballots and compulsory postal ballots for union elections, but other, more dubious, reforms outlawed what had formerly been widely accepted as legitimate union behaviour and removed specific individual protections.

Murray knew that the government would press on unless the unions acted firmly to put their own dishevelled house in order. He was a bureaucrat by training, no natural front man. He tried patiently and cautiously to edge the unions towards prudent reasonableness, while too often feeling it necessary publicly to promote TUC views which he was privately aware were moonshine.

Murray was saddled with a leadership vacuum among the big unions and hence on the TUC General Council. The TGWU's Moss Evans, in a different league to Jones, was pleasantly ineffectual. There were hopes that David Basnett, of the General and Municipal Workers' Union, would fill the gap, but his languid and equivocal approach was utterly inadequate. The electricians' Frank Chapple was by far the most able leader of a big union, but his rumbustious and irrepressible right-wing drumbeat enraged his enemies and scared off potential collaborators with less stomach than him for unpalatable impeachment of the unions' dangerous nonsense. Murray was hamstrung by a TUC hierarchy which was as much concerned with its own infighting as with the continuing external legislative omens.

The Conservatives were victorious again in the general election of 1983. Labour's doldrums meant no respite for the unions from Tory laws. They must learn to live within a statutory framework which the nation had endorsed at the polls. That was Murray's view. He made a spirited, if belated, attempt at the first TUC conference after the election to bang heads together and to demand a 'new realism'. The blinkered brothers thought otherwise, however, and Murray's impact was shortlived, as the ranting Arthur Scargill's mobocracy came increasingly into ascendancy.

It was not just Scargill, already willing his miners' union to disaster. Murray was roundly attacked by the TUC Left for refusing to back illegal action by the print union, the National Graphical Association (NGA), in its vicious dispute with provincial newspaper owner Eddie Shah. He was severely undermined too, by Mrs Thatcher's unwarranted and dunderheaded brush-off when he sought to promote a compromise agreement over the government ban on trade unionism at the GCHQ Cheltenham intelligence base. Perhaps the last straw for Murray was the TUC's stupid tit-for-tat decision to withdraw its representatives from Neddy (the National Economic Development Council), one of the few remaining tripartite bodies left intact by a government that was anxious to eliminate union input wherever possible. This pointless union protest action over the GCHQ fiasco destroyed Murray's faltering attempts to keep a toehold in Whitehall so that he could put the union case to whoever might still listen.

The unions' momentous own goals came as unemployment soared, sapping their membership and consequently their resources. Murray, drained and frustrated, opted for early retirement and duly collected his seat in the House of Lords. He left behind a trade union movement that matched his personal low spirits and morale. Things could only get better – or so it seemed. Instead, the unions lurched to dispiriting new depths.

The TUC under Willis

Norman Willis inherited from Murray the herculean task of jerking the unions back from self-destruction towards confident viability – a task in which he has so far been signally unsuccessful.

Willis's rambling and uncertain public performances have brought searing criticism, not least from within the General Council. There have been backstairs moves to depose him and he cannot avoid his share of the blame for the TUC's continuing decline. In 1990, the TUC-affiliated unions plunged into the red by around £25 million. Their debt-ridden state showed no marked improvement last year (1991). The twelve million membership peak of 1979 dropped to below ten million by 1985, and is now around eight million – probably far fewer if non-existent members, still on the books of many unions, are discounted. Significantly, non-unionists now form a clear majority of the nation's workforce. All this is reflected in the TUC's current parlous financial condition. Willis has been forced into a painful cost-cutting exercise at Congress House to keep the TUC afloat.

It is hard to pick out any genuine successes during the Willis stewardship. The failures abound: the TUC's flawed and hypocritical behaviour during the savagery of the miners' and print workers' strikes; the abortive bid to stop unions from taking government cash to pay for their ballots; the EETPU's expulsion from the TUC; the ban on strike-free deals. TUC-initiated recruitment drives have yielded little. It would, however, be a mistake to blame Willis, a decent, friendly and intelligent man, for all the current ills of the TUC, although it is unfortunate that he cannot impose any authority on the General Council. Today's situation exposes the inherent weakness of the TUC's top bureaucrat who must depend upon a few strong and trusty union barons if he is to achieve his objectives. That baronial backbone no longer exists. The big men, running the big unions, are missing.

TUC personalities

The General Council itself is a study in mediocrity. The unions send a generally uninspiring bunch to Congress House to represent them. Ron Todd, who heads the TGWU, is fairly typical. He is an oldfashioned bargainer, noted more for his broad shoulders and stentorian voice than for his qualities of leadership. The TGWU's thirty-nine-member executive council has been under Hard Left majority control for years, and Todd has been their captive. He has been severely embarrassed by rigged ballots which have helped to sustain the TGWU militants, while the union has become a financial and organizational disaster. A membership drive targeted at part-timers, women and young workers, has failed dismally. The buck stops with Todd, now on the verge of retirement.

The other big battalions are little better for positive leadership. John Edmonds, of the General, Municipal and Boilermakers' Union, is Oxford-educated, a self-declared 'centrist', and supposedly supplies the TUC's intellectual input. It is hard to discover. His union has grown through mergers with other unions, such as the boilermakers, but Edmonds' systematic opposition to the EETPU's strike-free deals, while quietly approving similar arrangements for his own members, is as depressing as it is revealing.

The Amalgamated Engineering Union (AEU) President, Bill Jordan, is down-to-earth and usually tries to inject reason into unreasonable TUC colleagues. However, he lacks the drive and charisma which might otherwise propel him into a more prominent role. Moreover, his flirtations with the unrepentant EETPU over a potential merger have frightened off possible allies. The AEU's prickly but able General Secretary, Gavin Laird, is kept off the General Council by petty jealousies within his own union's executive council.

The more talented union leaders are to be found among the middle-size and smaller white-collar organizations. Their occasional cries for sanity are muffled by the offbeat chorus of their bigger brothers. Todd, Edmonds, Ken Gill, Manufacturing, Science and Finance's cold-eyed commissar, also about to retire, the long-winded Rodney Bickerstaffe, of the National Union of Public Employees, avuncular Jimmy Knapp, of the Rail, Maritime and Transport Union, Alan Jinkinson, from NALGO (the local government workers' union), and the postmen's Alan Tuffin, together keep the TUC carthorse plodding aimlessly along its slow leftward path towards the knacker's yard.

The TUC has, however, gained one advantage, which is the relegation to the lunatic fringe of Arthur Scargill, whose sanctimonious pronouncements have been muted since the wounding repercussions throughout the National Union of Mineworkers of the calamitous miners' strike.

It is unfortunate that the vastly improved pay and conditions for union officials and staff over the past twenty years or so has not resulted in more proficient, if not dynamic, top people. Here and there, there is hope. Within Congress House, Willis's deputy, John Monks, level-headed ex-chief of the TUC organization department, is a good prospect. But the major manual workers' unions, in particular, remain in a time-warp.

New-style unionism

Outside the TUC, Eric Hammond, the electricians' iconoclast, is the undisputed leader of the pack. Even Hammond's General Council foes reluctantly admit to some admiration for his tenacious individualism. Not that they mourn the departure from their ranks of such an uncomfortable bedfellow – kicked off the General Council when the TUC expelled the EETPU. The truculent Hammond had the temerity to make them think.

Hammond, like Todd and Gill, is due to retire soon. His union adversaries know that many of yesterday's Hammond heresies – and those of his predecessor, Frank Chapple – are today's conventional TUC wisdom. Todd, Edmonds and Co. openly despised the EETPU's so-called business unionism – the plastic cards, cheap mortgages and bargain offers for the members. Now such advantages are TUC-sponsored as unions tout desperately for custom among a mostly resistant non-union labour force.

Hammond has cut away the pretence and accepted the inevitability of a decline in solidarity between groups of workers. It was clear during the last big coal strike that the electricians, the dockers, the lorry drivers and the steel workers did not identify with the miners' cause. The EETPU alone balloted its electricity industry members to prove the point.

The electricians, set free in 1961 from the control of Communist ballot-riggers, went on to pioneer postal balloting for their members. It followed that they had no anxiety about the Conservative government's provisions for statutory balloting procedures, as they voluntarily made extensive use of the ballot box to bypass the activist minority and to secure the views of the wider membership.

Results of Conservative industrial legislation

Government measures have introduced members of all unions to ballot-box democracy, and they like it. No future government will dare to remove what is now an enshrined principle and practical necessity for the British trade union movement.

Many trade unionists undoubtedly believe that Conservative legislation has been too blatantly anti-union to be fair, but they are unimpressed by TUC blanket opposition to every new employment law, including the balloting requirements. They have lived with the consequences of flawed and feudal union democracy, Scargill-style, and with the kind of fraudulent voting systems revealed in the squalid manœuvrings within the TGWU. Even the TUC has got that message, and its outright antagonism has abated.

Trade unions have no God-given right to exist. It is not enough to recall their history of courageous resistance to persecution and oppression while establishing the right to organize. Such struggles, however virtuous, are long gone. Unions must now earn the respect and support of free men and women. Conscription into their ranks wanes fast as the closed shop is whittled away, again by statute.

Recession has shattered union membership, especially in its traditional manufacturing industry stronghold. The sociological pattern of union membership has changed drastically as more and more union members see themselves as middle class. Three-quarters of them own their own homes or are buying them on mortgages. Many are share-owners. Working wives, two-car families, holidays abroad, have created the necessity for a new kind of trade unionism which can respond flexibly to the continuing changes in our industrial and social structure, including the inexorable switch of emphasis from manufacturing to service industry. The unions can no longer take their members for granted.

Those members will not accept the kind of mindless and indiscriminate opposition to the government which featured throughout the eighties. Trade union members resented being used as political lobby fodder. Many of them showed it by voting Tory or for the SDP–Liberal Alliance. Conservative ministers welcomed over-zealous and ill-contrived union defiance as a political bonus. None of this helped unions to gain or to retain members in an inhospitable world. Even unions which reject an outdated, class-based approach have suffered. Public opinion is mostly unable to distinguish between the good guys and the bad guys. The smear is unrefined.

There is of course another side to the story. Unions do remain a source of moral values in society, despite their more obvious and multi-faceted failings. Their antiquated structures have been allowed to stagnate by lethargic members, and that is a common enough phenomenon in all democratic institutions, especially familiar to

11

those who seek reform of our anomalous first-past-the-post electoral system.

Unions are mainly run by people who, whatever their politics, want to improve the lot of their fellow trade unionists and usually of all of us. They speak out legitimately and usefully in areas beyond the narrow confines of wages and conditions – on health and safety, on the environment, on transport, on regional development. They should do so more often, more purposefully, drawing on the first-hand wide-ranging experience of their members. They can properly contribute to the arguments about employee share-ownership and profit-sharing and should be positively involved in the evolving Euro-economy.

Unions are, however, only part of the industrial equation. Employers cannot avoid their share of the blame for the labour scene's short-comings. Too many anti-union employers use the admitted excesses of union militants to pretend that all unions are undesirables to be shunned, rather than encouraged. Employers, including the government, should do far more than pay lip-service to the gains of working together with unions in productive partnership. Unions can provide an effective channel of communication with employees which can save companies from otherwise sizeable investment in management time and training.

The unions will not vanish but they are in a backs-to-the-wall fight for a worthwhile future. Most of them appear to be ill-suited to and ill at ease in a modern industrial environment in which their power is strictly limited. Some of them seem dangerously content to await the return of a Labour government, which they fondly believe will reinstate them to a privileged position. It is a high-risk strategy, as Labour – in the event of it regaining power – is unlikely to undo too much of the Conservatives' industrial legislation.

Mrs Thatcher boasted that she gave the unions back to their members. That is not fully proven, but her ballot reforms are an undeniable and memorable advance. She compelled the unions to do what they had foolishly and wilfully refused to do voluntarily. For them, the preservation of time-worn rule books and self-interest were more important than the best interests of their members. But the members are the movement. As the ballot box becomes an increasingly familiar tool in their working lives they may yet shake up the established and archaic behavioural norms of their various organizations.

Members have a far greater chance than ever before to participate directly in creating the unions of their choice. Experience teaches slowly. Have the led learned from the past mistakes of their leaders? Will they seize the opportunity, or will apathy, the old enemy of progress, hold sway? Even cautious optimism is barely justified so far. It would, though, be richly ironic if Margaret Thatcher, through her ballot reforms, proved to be the unwitting saviour of the very institutions which she sought to crush.

2

Block Votes and Ballot-Rigging

The period from 1960 has often seemed like a thirty-year war of attrition between the unions and the rest of British society. Likewise, the unions' fratricidal relationship with Labour – the party which they founded to represent working people in parliament.

The sixties were tempestuous years for industry. Masterful unions demanded and secured their say in government decision-taking on issues ranging far beyond the bread-and-butter concerns and requirements of their members. They were into everything: defence and disarmament; foreign policy; immigration; health; housing; Northern Ireland. From the atom to Zimbabwe, the unions presumptuously pronounced with the minimum of qualification, preparation or consultation with those for whom they presumed to speak.

It was not that they should have refrained from advancing a viewpoint on behalf of the unionized workforce, however dubious their groundwork and intellectual capacity. Their mistake was their insistence that Labour, in particular, should do far more than simply take note of what they had to say. Unions throughout the Western democratic world are of course politically involved. They back parties, endorse candidates and finance campaigns. But the British Labour Party has an overriding constitutional link, especially through the unions' block vote control of the annual party conference. It is an undemocratic, unrepresentative and unhealthy situation. The unions are primarily in business to promote sectional interests, worthy or not. They have too often been allowed to come perilously close to dictating government policy – and on occasion have managed to do so.

Labour has begun to recognize the unappealing nature of all this to the public. It seeks gradually to reduce the relevance of the union block

14

vote to its procedures and policies, to create a more arms-length affair, perhaps in keeping with that between the Democratic Party and organized labour in the United States. Its hesitancy is understandable, if not excusable. The unions are crucial to the party's funding, and if Labour's union paymasters do not call the policy tune, they will be less willing to pay the piper. It is probable too, that a downturn in union activity would leave a gap too easily filled by constituency party militants. Labour proceeds with caution, but it would seem that change is on the way.

My own industrial reporting began with the vain attempt by the Labour Leader, Hugh Gaitskell, to thwart the TGWU's Frank Cousins and the nuclear disarmers at the 1960 Labour conference in Scarborough. My reporting days ended ten years later with the Labour government's fall in the wake of its debilitating clash with the unions over 'In Place of Strife', its ill-fated plan to stop unofficial strikes and to curb the unions.

Between these dramatic events came:

(1) Harold Wilson's election victories of 1964 and 1966 and the perpetual economic quagmire through which his governments struggled;

(2) the unions' lurch from co-operation with Wilson over pay policy, to 'reluctant acquiescence' and then to burning hostility;

(3) the unprecedented Electrical Trades Union ballot rigging trial in the High Court, followed by the overthrow of that union's corrupt Communist regime;

(4) the crippling seamen's strike against Labour's pay policy, denounced by Prime Minister Wilson as a Communist-inspired plot.

It was the heyday of the labour and industrial correspondent (the title varied according to the newspaper), the specialist journalists who offered their colourful blow-by-blow accounts of industry's constant discord. It was the unions that provided the bulk of the best copy, not least centred on their love–hate relationship with Labour. These were the stories with 'blood' on them which editors reckoned interested their readers and were sure fascinated their mostly right-wing proprietors. They readily 'splashed' such stories, and huge banner headlines regularly proclaimed the Labour movement's ill-concealed divisions.

Those union block votes not only resolved the party conference position on key issues. They commanded the majority of seats on the

15

party's National Executive Committee, its ruling body between conferences. Behind the scenes, the unions were the king-makers when a political crown was at stake. Their clout extended significantly into the Parliamentary Labour Party, where union-sponsored MPs were a sizeable force to be reckoned with. Above all, union money allowed them to pull the political strings.

The industrial correspondent was the man (and, occasionally, woman) on the union beat. Union leaders became intimates, sometimes friends. They used the industrial reporting corps, mostly broadly sympathetic to the unions, to get their case over to the public and often for personal public relations. Electioneering union leaders assiduously cultivated those whose newspaper reports might influence their members' votes. There was usually a return, however, and the journalists winkled out information about the mainly secretive unions' internal affairs that was never intended for wider scrutiny. It was a kind of unwritten bargain, one which the undefatigable union bargainers understood and welcomed.

It followed that the industrial correspondents covered the business of Labour's National Executive Committee where the union writ ran large. Woe betide the political hack who strayed across the demarcation line. The place for political correspondents was at Westminster and even at the party conference they were expected to play second fiddle to the industrial supremos.

The party's senior politicians, keen to propagate their views rather than leave the field to their union counterparts, were also ready to treat with the industrial reporters. The firm theory among the political journalists was that most of the leaks which poured from the National Executive Committee about their oh-so-secret deliberations came from the union members of that untrustworthy body. Most journalists had their own pet contacts and the industrials veered towards union sources. But the politicos were ready to blow the gaff and whisper away to the industrials when it suited them.

That Labour's National Executive Committee is now the hunting ground of the political reporters is less a reflection of any fundamental change in Labour's structure than a consequence of the steady decline in the relative importance of the industrial journalist's job. That decline got under way in the early seventies, as national newspapers trimmed their staff and sought to 'rationalize' coverage, and was compounded during the Thatcher years. Union power has been emaciated, mirrored by the limited space now given to union affairs in the press, on television and on radio, and by the parallel downgrading of the industrial reporter's role.

Labour, the unions and the Bomb

Labour's annual conferences are always tumultuous and usually have as much to do with comradeship as a KGB convention. Even so, the 1960 gathering ranks as the most electrifying and deeply passionate of all, including even those which, years later, spawned the Social Democrats' break from Labour and posed the greatest ever threat to the party's existence. This was the climax to the Gaitskellite versus Bevanite war that raged within the Labour Party throughout the fifties. German rearmament was followed by Britain's decision to manufacture the H-bomb. Labour's anguish and perpetual disorder helped to keep the Conservatives in office from 1951. Attlee resigned as Labour leader after the party's 1955 election defeat. Gaitskell beat Aneurin Bevan to become the new leader, but by 1957 Bevan had shifted sufficiently to dismay his left-wing supporters and argue against unilateral nuclear disarmament. Britain, he said, in his famous speech, could not go 'naked into the conference chamber'.

The Conservative Party won its third successive and its biggest post-war election victory in 1959. Harold Macmillan persuaded the nation that it had 'never had it so good'. Labour stumbled deeper into its ideologically based and violently divisive fracas over nuclear weapons.

Those slugging it out at Scarborough in 1960 could not have foreseen that the nuclear issue would remain alive within the party, like a deadly disease, sometimes virulent, sometimes dormant, for some thirty years more. Gaitskell certainly realized that defence and disarmament were all-important to Labour's immediate future.

Bevan's enormous influence had gone. He died in the summer of 1960. The union block votes could no longer be counted on to rally behind the party leaders. The 1956 election of Frank Cousins to head the TGWU brought an extraordinary change. The TGWU under Ernest Bevin, then under Arthur Deakin, was the bulwark on which rested Labour moderation – or right-wing authoritarianism, as the Left contended with some justification. Cousins transformed the situation and destabilized both the TUC and the Labour Party.

'The Big Fella', as he was known to his officials, dropped on an unsuspecting trade union movement like the H-bomb he so vehemently decried. He was catapulted into office by the deaths, in rapid succession, of Deakin and his immediate successor, Jock Tiffin. Cousins took over when much of the TGWU activist membership was ripe for release from the interminable smothering embrace of their right-wing leadership. From the outset Cousins declared his abhorrence of wage restraint and heralded the end of TUC co-operation with the Conservative government over economic affairs. His attitude on pay contained an implicit warning to any future Labour government that might wish to tamper with free collective bargaining.

Cousins towered over the trade union scene, physically and through the force of his contribution. No single trade union leader, before or since, has produced his virtual revolution in established trade union policy and practice. Nor has any union leader reproduced the direct, if mostly unwelcome, effect that his leftwards drive had upon the Labour government of the day. Cousins had emerged as the premier spokesman for the nuclear disarmers, eclipsing the political Left and pulling his own TGWU biennial policy conference in 1959 behind the ban-the-bomb approach. The 1960 TUC faced both ways – supporting both the Cousins line and official Labour policy. This was largely due to the crafty manœuvres of Bill (later Lord) Carron, President of the Amalgamated Engineering Union and ardent Gaitskellite, who per-suaded his muddled delegates to back both viewpoints.

By the time Labour's conference gathered in Scarborough in the autumn of 1960, Gaitskell's leadership was on the line, and so was Labour's future. There was exceptional tension in the pre-conference meetings of the National Executive Committee and in the union delegations where the block votes were to be horse-traded.

There was a serious setback for Gaitskell before the conference opened. The National Executive Committee voted narrowly that conference policy decisions should bind the Parliamentary Party. It was one more foolhardy decree that was to run and run, always to Labour's public embarrassment. Meanwhile, Campaign for Nuclear Disarma-ment demonstrators marched and chanted 'Gaitskell must go' outside the Scarborough hotel where the party leaders were in session. The National Executive Committee backed Gaitskell but it was already apparent that the bulk of the block votes were committed against him.

On the eve of the nuclear debate journalists thronged the doorstep of the local public library where the AEU delegation was in session. Bill Carron was up to his tricks again. The rotund little Roman Catholic, known as 'The Cardinal', was engaged in a last fling to try and rescue Gaitskell. Once again he tried to persuade his delegates to vote both ways. But this bunch was more left-wing and less naive than those at the TUC conference. They voted by a 2–1 majority for the anti-nuclear policy. Gaitskell's last fragile hope had gone.

Next day at the Spa Grand Hall, Cousins put the TGWU case with force. Carron refused to speak for his delegation, and it was left to a worthily dull rank-and-file delegate, Len Misledine, to represent the AEU at the rostrum. There was only one speech that mattered. Gaitskell could not win the vote, but he was determined to win the argument. His was a spellbinding performance, one of the all-time great orations of British politics. He infuriated his opponents by dubbing them 'fellow-travellers' and pro-Communist stool-pigeons, linking unilateralism firmly with neutralism. It was his peroration that blazed the message that the battle was lost but Labour's ferocious civil war was far from over. He put fresh heart into his hitherto dispirited supporters. 'There are some of us who will fight, fight and fight again to save the party we love', he declared unforgettably. 'We will fight, fight and fight again to bring back sanity and honesty and dignity so that our party, with its great past, may retain its glory and its greatness.' There were few hard-faced cynics in the press seats that day. It was an heroic effort and was widely recognized as such. The crusade was under way from that moment. The union block votes were the target. They had to be shifted during the next year's summer conference season.

The breakthrough began at the AEU's 1961 policy-making National Committee in Eastbourne, and with USDAW, the shopworkers' union, gathered in Bournemouth at the same time. The nuclear issue was due to be decided towards the end of the two-week-long AEU meeting. There were fewer than seventy delegates in those days, and Carron and his chief lieutenant, John (later Sir John) Boyd, worked feverishly to get a moderate majority. At Bournemouth, too, strenuous efforts were afoot to swing USDAW from unilateralism. USDAW voted for change – the first clear indication that the unilateralists' supremacy would be shortlived, that they were heading back to a political wilderness which they were to occupy for more than twenty years before they again prevailed. Now the AEU, followed by the miners and the railwaymen, joined the growing Gaitskellite bandwagon.

Cousins kept his grip on the TGWU despite fevered attempts by Gaitskell's campaigners to overthrow his policy within his own stronghold. Labour's Deputy Leader, George Brown, was a TGWU-sponsored MP and was once a junior official in the union – a fact he used frequently to establish his trade union credentials.

19

Brown was refused permission by the TGWU leadership to address the union's 800-strong biennial delegate conference in Brighton, so he set up his own fringe meeting in a local theatre. There was a large crop of anti-Cousins motions on the conference agenda and a fair number of delegates who would back them. But trade unionists are always suspicious of outside interference and Brown's meeting was seen as just that. Thanks to the press presence, his tiny audience was more than doubled. The delegates stayed away. Inside the TGWU conference, Cousins steamrollered his way to a 3–1 majority and a standing ovation.

This time though, the block votes elsewhere were committed against him. The 1961 TUC in Portsmouth, where George Woodcock made his debut as General Secretary, gave Gaitskell a thumping majority on nuclear policy. A month later, at Labour's Blackpool conference, Cousins's attempt to resell the anti-nuclear gospel brought him the slow handclap. Gaitskell got a huge ovation and a majority to match.

The nuclear debate has never ceased to burden Labour. Left-wing dedication and guile turned Labour back to its bad old ways in the eighties. Gaitskell's kind of fight resumed, but in a far more guarded and apologetic fashion. Neil Kinnock, one-time ardent nuclear disarmer, has belatedly recognized that Gaitskell and his own idol, Bevan, were right. Labour again claims to be multilateralist, but its policy blur makes it an uncertain proposition, with echoes of the AEU's two-way stance back in 1960.

The ETU: Cannon, Chapple and the Communists

The early sixties saw too the climax of what Gerald Gardiner, QC (later a Labour Lord Chancellor) called 'the biggest fraud in the history of British trade unionism'. This was the Communist Party plot to maintain its iron control of the Electrical Trades Union.

A small group of anti-Communists, spearheaded by ex-Communists Les Cannon and Frank Chapple, had battled since 1957 to prove that ETU elections were rigged. In 1961 they went to the High Court to obtain a declaration that the 1959 election for General Secretary was null and void – that the Communist Frank Haxell was not properly re-elected against the challenge of John 'Jock' Byrne.

Byrne, the union's West-of-Scotland area official, was co-plaintiff in the court action with Chapple. Byrne, a staunch Roman Catholic and Labour man, had stood unsuccessfully for national office on and off since 1947. Now his prolonged and courageous tenacity was to be rewarded.

Mr Justice Winn delivered his historic 40,000-word judgment: that the ETU was managed and controlled by Communists and pliant sympathizers in the interests of the Communist Party; that Haxell, Frank Foulkes, the union's President, and other senior figures, had conspired to stop Byrne's election by fraud and unlawful devices. It spelled the end for the ETU's corrupt Communist rulers. Subsequently, the judge ruled that Byrne was the union's elected General Secretary and that elections for a new Executive Council should be held. Those elections were to be free from any Communist influence. Thus the Communist Party lost the jewel in its industrial crown, and never regained it.

Haxell was a cold fish whose demolition brought few regrets on personal grounds, even from the Left, despite the immense political setback which the whole affair represented for them. Foulkes was a different proposition. He was an affable drinking companion with a dry humour which went down well with the gullible leaders of other unions and notably with the left-wing cronies whom he entertained liberally at the expense of the ETU's members. There was great reluctance to believe the allegations against him. Cannon and Chapple were branded as turncoats and upstarts by much of the trade union establishment. The TUC sat timidly on its hands rather than dirty them by the kind of punitive involvement which the blatant lies and evasions of Foulkes, Haxell and their ETU politburo had long demanded. Inside the TUC's Congress House headquarters, Victor Feather, several rungs down the hierarchical ladder when the ETU campaign began, was almost a lone sympathizer with the anti-Communists.

Cannon and Chapple were an acquired taste, but they should nevertheless rate high on any trade union roll of honour. Cannon was the dominant member of the duo. He possessed an arrogant intellect that in argument could be smooth or savage. He stoked up the envy and embitterment of his political enemies who could rarely match his energy, cunning and foresight. Cannon broke with the Communists over the 1956 Hungarian uprising. Soon after, they sacked him from his job as the union's Education Officer. Once Foulkes was deposed, Cannon, the chief architect of his downfall, was the natural successor as President.

Cannon went on to set the pace for the reform and modernization of the union. (I went swimming with Cannon, by then Sir Leslie, at the

21

1970 Labour conference in Blackpool. There was then no hint of the tragedy to come, but within months, he was dead from cancer.) Had he lived longer, he would doubtless have cemented his standing as one of the foremost constructive thinkers and doers in post-war British trade unionism – unless he had succumbed to one of the tempting offers from industry which he told me that until then he had steadfastly refused.

Frank Chapple was a very different character, every bit as pugnacious as Cannon but more volatile. (First impressions tended to cast him as something of an East End roughneck.) With Cannon's death, Chapple emerged in a similarly masterful position within the union. If Cannon started the union's process of fundamental change, Chapple did far more than consolidate it. He was the generator of today's EETPU, as it is now called, which justifiably claims to be Britain's most democratic and streamlined union. Chapple's long run at the top of his union and in the senior councils of the Labour movement was riddled with controversy. Yet even his most fervent critics on the TUC General Council conceded that his eventual chairmanship of that body was highly efficient and uncharacteristically impartial.

Chapple was full of personality contradictions. He talked tough but was erudite. He could be crude and chauvinistic, but many of those with whom he clashed admit to receiving his quiet helping hand when in trouble. He was not a man to hold personal grudges. At the TUC he was scathing in his dismissal of the mealy-mouthed nonsense that has done so much harm to our unions. Chapple was a members' General Secretary, ever seeking to reflect the viewpoint of the ordinary members who elected him.

The ETU's Communist activists contaminated the entire Labour movement. They and their apologists deserved no sympathy. But the anti-Communists had strains among themselves with which they had to cope. Byrne was highly suspicious of Cannon and Chapple, and found it hard to come to terms with their Communist pasts. There were some nasty moments within the anti-Communist ranks before Cannon became their presidential candidate. Still, the anti-Communists held together. The retired Lord Chapple is the only major figure from the old ETU scandal who is still around. He rarely takes his seat in the House of Lords, and that is their lordships' loss.

Chapple's successors in the union stand by the fiddle-proof postal balloting system for union elections, independently supervised, that was perhaps the single most important outcome of the exposure of the Communists' villainy. It was here that the seed was sown for the broad reform of union balloting procedures which has been one of the most desirable elements of Conservative legislation in the eighties. It might never have happened but for that desperate but determined fight against the odds and the strength of character shown by Cannon, Chapple, Byrne, and their handful of active supporters, some thirty years earlier. Theirs was a real and lasting achievement, built upon by others but originally secured by guts, sacrifice and the diligent perseverance more commonly associated with the zealots of the Left.

Macmillan, the unions and the ascendancy of Wilson

The fifties were presented by Prime Minister Macmillan as the boom years, concealing the chronic failure to modernize and re-equip British industry and to train and retrain its workforce. (History has repeated itself during the Thatcher years.)

The TUC's generally co-operative strategy with the government on the economic front was shattered by Cousins who insisted: 'In a period of freedom for all, we are part of the all.' These were words which he repeated many times in his stubbornly consistent rejection of wage restraint.

By 1961 Macmillan's Chancellor, Selwyn Lloyd, grappled with recession, with an escalating balance of payments problem and with rising unemployment. Lloyd sought wage curbs and tried to placate the unions by establishing Neddy (the National Economic Development Council) to bring government, employers and unions together on a regular basis to discuss the nation's difficulties and to try to thrash out solutions. All Cousins's suspicions were aroused but Woodcock took a more sanguine view. He wanted the TUC centre stage in dealing with the economy. Moreover, he was cajoling and persuading big unions outside the TUC – NALGO, the local government officers, and the National Union of Teachers – to affiliate. They were averse to any pro-Labour political links. They wanted the TUC to concentrate on industrial matters and were impressed by the opportunity for unions to influence the government directly through TUC participation in Neddy.

Woodcock frowned unceasingly beneath his bushy eyebrows in the frustration he shared with all TUC general secretaries who have tried to make the unions square up to realities. If anyone could persuade the prickly Cousins to relent, it was Woodcock. The two men worked well together and respected each other. They also had in common their contempt for most other TUC General Council members. Woodcock privately regarded the majority of his TUC colleagues as boneheaded artisans, incapable of intelligent decision-making. He had a point, but his disdain was so transparent that it was counter-productive to his aims. His attitude towards Cousins was markedly different. He talked Cousins round. The TGWU leader not only withdrew his opposition to Neddy but became a TUC-nominated member.

Selwyn Lloyd started on the incomes policy road that has brought successive governments grave conflict and ultimate disaster. It was a tentative enough beginning. Wages were not to rise by more than 2.5 per cent annually on average for each worker – the so-called 'guiding light'. That was soon breached, however, when the port employers, threatened with a national dock strike by the truculent TGWU, caved in and conceded more pay and shorter hours, worth twice the government's norm.

Lloyd did not last much longer. Macmillan's 'Night of the Long Knives' in July 1962 found the Chancellor among nearly a third of the Cabinet that was sacked. Macmillan went on to launch Nicky (the National Incomes Commission), a watchdog tribunal aimed at maintaining the government's grip on pay. The new body would take 'the national interest' into account when looking at claims. It was, however, more of a lapdog than a watchdog – a creature of the government. This time Woodcock and Cousins agreed on a non-cooperation policy, and easily carried the TUC with them.

That same year saw another surprise event – a reconciliation between Gaitskell and Cousins over the Common Market. Gaitskell's speech at Labour's annual conference was a forthright rejection of Macmillan's attempts at EEC entry. Cousins was delighted. (Some years later he told me that Gaitskell even sounded him out about joining a future Labour government. 'I didn't say "yes" and I didn't say "no" ,' he said.)

Within months of this unexpected meeting of minds, Gaitskell was dead. It was 1963, the next general election neared and leadership was crucial. Despite the implacable hostility of Labour's right-wingers, Harold Wilson defeated George Brown and James Callaghan to take over as leader. Cousins and the Left supported Wilson as the candidate most likely to deliver their requirements if elected. The Wilson of those days was a compulsive performer. Audiences hung on his syllables and chortled at his beautifully timed wisecracks. More importantly, he offered hope of a fairer Britain, built on a much-needed new economic dynamism, coupled with social justice.

Another major industrial controversy was to break in 1963: the Beeching Plan. Dr Richard Beeching (later Lord Beeching) was in charge of the railways with a brief from Macmillan and his Transport Minister, Ernest Marples, to modernize, come what may, and this meant swingeing cuts in services and jobs.

'Dr Beeching', I wrote in the *Daily Express*, 'abandoned his bedside manner with Britain's sick railways and set about them with a gigantic axe.' The cuts really were massive – 150,000 jobs to go over seven years, more than half the passenger stations and lines to close, and the end for the bulk of the existing freight depots. Beeching's comment, 'Generally there is a great emotional upsurge when we close a service. A week or two afterwards the whole thing dies away', was tactless and insensitive. It underlined the justifiable view of the unions that this was a severe and unrelenting man, a technocrat with scant concern for the human consequences of his actions.

The Tory government was more and more jaded. Nicky was a failure. Reginald Maudling, the new Chancellor, tried a 3–5.5 per cent 'guiding light' which flickered fitfully. Unemployment headed for a million and reached a record level before turning downwards again. But the government's troubles were not only economic. Two journalists went to prison for refusing to divulge sources of information to Lord Radcliffe's tribunal of inquiry into security lapses arising from the case of the Admiralty clerk, John Vassall, jailed for eighteen years for spying. The media, disenchanted with Macmillan and impressed by the dexterous Wilson, were outraged by what was seen as a government-inspired attack on the press through two men who were simply obeying the rules of their craft. Journalists cannot be above the law but the government, suffering already from a severe media mauling, was out for revenge. Even the Tory *Daily Express* declared:

Respectable men are being sent to prison because they are loyal to their professional code of conduct. Is that code wrong? It is devised in the public interest. Are journalists asking for a right which should not be conceded to them? They believe – every newspaperman in Britain believes – that this right is essential to the efficient working of a democracy.

There was worse to come for Macmillan. Before the Vassal Tribunal issued its report a far greater sex and security scandal engulfed the government – the Profumo affair. The cumulative effect on the Macmillan administration of this and so many other economic and social setbacks indicated a government on the ropes and heading for the count.

Macmillan's departure and replacement by Sir Alec Douglas Home offered no respite. Douglas Home was no match for the wiles, repartee and razor-sharp political cutting edge of Wilson, revelling in his mastery, both inside and outside the House of Commons.

Not that all Wilson's domestic worries had vanished. Labour and the unions were by no means all sweetness and light. Cousins remained adamantly opposed to an incomes policy which Labour politicians now began to see as a vital ingredient in their alternative economic strategy.

Wilson came clean at the TGWU's 1963 biennial policy conference at Scarborough. He offered the unions a partnership with a Labour government. Then he said firmly: 'We shall have to ask for restraint in the matter of incomes. But we mean all incomes. . . .' Restraint would be part of a socially just economic policy, based on expansion. Cousins, victim of a heart attack, was not at the conference. His second-in-command, Harry Nicholas, was an effective deputy. There was no dissent at Wilson's message; far from it. He won three standing ovations.

Cousins was back in harness for the September TUC conference. Now he clashed sharply with his customary ally, Woodcock. Inevitably, it was over pay policy. Woodcock wanted to present a document to the delegates which logically accepted the consideration of wages as part of any overall economic plan, whatever the government. After fierce backstage arguments, Woodcock capitulated. Or did he? His resolute speech to the conference effectively reinstated the vetoed parts of the document. Any government, he asserted, had to take a view on wages and the unions must respond if they wanted other things to be planned. The unions, he declaimed, had 'left Trafalgar Square' for the committee rooms of Whitehall. He was right in theory and in practice. An era of intimate trade union involvement in affairs of state was to follow. Cousins remained defiant. In an oft-repeated sentence, he told the conference: 'We will not have wage restraint, whoever brings it and wraps it up for us.'

There was a memorable and oft-repeated sentence too, at Labour's 1963 conference, again at Scarborough. It was here that Wilson talked of the white heat of the technological revolution or, to be accurate, of 'the Britain that is going to be forged in the white heat of this revolution'. He struck a chord which chimed with the nation's mood – the need for Britain to renovate, innovate, embrace social, industrial and technological change. It contrasted sharply with the tawdry Tory image.

The predominant theme of the conference was unity. Yet there were underlying strains which subsequently surfaced in an ugly fashion when Labour came to power. I led page one of the *Daily Express* on successive days with reports, not from the conference, but from fringe meetings. They were a graphic illustration of trouble ahead.

The first of my reports concerned a Wilson speech to a Fabian gathering. I wrote: 'Mr Harold Wilson revealed his intention last night of reshaping the administrative machine of government if the socialists gain power.' I said that the key would be a new Ministry of Production and Economic Planning which would 'overlord' the Treasury. I listed other new ministries to be created, including Overseas Development, headed by a minister of Cabinet rank. I reported that the proposed powers of the new economic ministry had already caused acute dissension among party chiefs.

That dissension emerged clearly enough twenty-four hours later, when James Callaghan, the Shadow Chancellor, spoke at a tea meeting and insisted on final Treasury reponsibility on vital economic issues. Jim knew that George Brown was earmarked for the economic ministry. He stressed that no final decisions had been taken and he added: 'It will be a great mistake if we try to blur the responsibility for these issues. We shall court trouble and difficulty if we do.' Prophetic words indeed. Those difficulties dogged Labour throughout the second half of the sixties. The Treasury and the Department of Economic Affairs, as the new ministry was eventually called, were permanently at loggerheads, as were their political bosses, Callaghan and Brown.

Callaghan had been stung to reply to Wilson by my newspaper story of the earlier meeting. He said: 'There ain't going to be no quarrel and there ain't going to be no enemies – and I hope that Lord Beaverbrook will make careful note of that before he invents any more trouble.' There was no invention and Jim knew it. But a spot of media-bashing has always been excellent cover for Labour politicians.

There was a significant event in late 1963 in the trade union personality stakes, though it was scarcely recognized as such at the time. Jack Jones was appointed to the No. 3 job in the TGWU. Both Cousins and his deputy, Harry Nicholas, had been on the sick list and both were due to retire in a little over six years if they went the full distance. So fifty-year-old Jones was already lined up for the top position. That was Cousins's deliberate intention. Jones, until then the union's Midlands regional secretary, was a long-standing political ally and friend of 'The Big Fella'. The post of Assistant Executive Secretary was dreamed up by Cousins and tailormade for Jones. He was selected by the TGWU Executive Council from a shortlist of nine, but there was never any doubt about the outcome. Cousins had done his fixing and the heir-apparent was in place.

Everything was building up towards a 1964 general election. Every union conference that summer became a rally for the Labour government to be. By the time Harold Wilson addressed the 1964 TUC conference in Blackpool even George Woodcock's customary political reserve had slipped. He openly confessed that he hoped for a Labour victory because another Tory government would be 'insufferable'. Wilson, for his part, pledged to restore those legal immunities to the unions which had been undermined by the Tories. He hammered home the partnership theme and once more asserted the need for an incomes policy within a socially just and equitable policy framework.

There was not much longer to wait. Labour's October poll triumph was a close-run thing – 317 seats for Labour, 303 for the Tories, nine for the Liberals. But the 'thirteen wasted years' of Conservative rule were over. The promised land beckoned.

Wilson's bold pre-election insistence on incomes policy was about to face its big test with the unions. The easy eloquence of opposition was to be replaced with the harsh reality of policy implementation.

3

Unions Rampant

These were heady days. Labour's spanking new 1964-registered vehicle careered along, never entirely out of control but always threatening to run out of road. Harold Wilson, aged forty-eight, moved quickly to implement his ambitious plans to recast the machinery of government. His famous first hundred days were action-packed – 'dynamic', as he had promised.

His Chancellor was James Callaghan. George Brown was First Secretary of State, in effect Deputy Prime Minister, and got what he craved for – command of the new Department of Economic Affairs (DEA). Frank Cousins was drafted in as Minister of Technology, another startling innovation. Barbara Castle was the first-ever Minister of Overseas Aid and Development, and had a Cabinet seat.

Cousins was readily given leave of absence from the TGWU and a Commons seat was found for him through a contrived by-election in the safe Labour berth of Nuneaton. Harry Nicholas took over as the TGWU's Acting General Secretary and Jack Jones moved up to be Acting Assistant General Secretary.

Wilson thought that the capture of Cousins would help him greatly with the unions, not least by taming their most bolshie left-winger. But Cousins was an uncomfortable Cabinet bedfellow, always prepared to be the odd man out. He was ill at ease in the Westminster political environment and, like others dropped in at the ministerial deep end without prior parliamentary experience, he found the Commons Despatch Box a place of torment and frustration. He was a commanding figure in the TGWU, but a cruelly exposed novice in the labyrinth of parliamentary convention and anachronism.

Labour's inherited problems defied all predictions. When the books were opened up there was a devastating £800 million balance of payments deficit – vast for those days. Wilson decided crucially against devaluation but a package of crisis economic measures was hurried in, including a 15 per cent import surcharge and massive foreign borrowing. This was swiftly followed by an emergency Budget.

Brown at the DEA

The unions were soon in the eye of the gathering storm. By December 1964, Brown, working with manic intensity, had concluded a series of soul-searching meetings with industrial leaders, culminating in the Declaration of Intent, a tripartite pledge by government, employers and unions to co-operate by voluntary methods to conquer wage and price inflation and to boost productivity.

The Prices and Incomes Board (the PIB), headed by Tory ex-minister Aubrey Jones, was established. Jones was a considerable gamble on Brown's part but he turned out to be an inspired choice. The PIB, under Jones, was fair, trustworthy and even-handed. Many of its reports were of lasting value. Few of those who attacked the government's prices and incomes policy were able to sustain a viable case against the PIB's scrupulous application of that policy. Initially, however, the PIB was toothless. Voluntarism was expected to be enough to keep prices stable and incomes down to a 3–3.5 per cent annual average increase. It was a vain hope.

Brown won overwhelming union support at the outset. Only the TGWU stood apart among the bigger organizations. Brown traversed the union conference circuit, ramming home his message. He prodded and teased a special conference of executive members of all the TUC-affiliated unions, meeting in London. Did they believe in order or chaos, planning or anarchy? Which offered Britain the way ahead? He was the government's super-salesman, peddling his wares with passion and conviction. 'I have no doubts, no misgivings, about commending the policy,' he said. It had nothing in common, he contended, with the crude wage restraint of previous Conservative governments.

Brown's tirades, indiscretions and non-conformist behaviour earned him constant headlines. But his courage and immense political skill showed through. At the Electrical Trades Union's conference at the Isle of Man, he emphasized that he was talking about 'the planned growth of real incomes'. That phrase echoed the Cousins line and was aimed more at 'The Big Fella' than at the ETU delegates. It was, said Brown, an essential part of the government's national plan for raising output by 25 per cent by 1970.

It was aspiring and audacious stuff. But the economic crisis worsened. By September 1965, Brown was at the TUC's Brighton conference to urge the unions to take a stiffer dose of medicine. The TGWU was set to fight his plan for the TUC to vet wage claims. The ETU opposed it too, for very different reasons. The electricians remained frozen out from a TUC General Council seat, a legacy of the ill will within the TUC hierarchy at the temerity of Cannon, Chapple and Co. in using the courts to kick out the Communists. The ETU's retaliatory response was that it wanted no TUC meddling with its interests, a sign of things to come a quarter of a century later. It would discuss its claims direct with the PIB, if necessary, and still backed the overall incomes policy.

Brown also planned an 'early warning' system for wage and price rises and powers for the PIB to delay increases while it investigated. The TUC's own fire-fighting arrangement would underpin all this but it was clear that voluntarism was on the way out. There were hours of anxious argument and toing and froing between Brown and the TUC leaders before he secured their agreement and, in turn, that of the conference. The TGWU led an opposition which was to expand steadily and it was known that Cousins was a rogue elephant within the Cabinet.

Wilson and Cousins

Labour's conference in Blackpool a month later offered proof positive about Cousins. It was a remarkable spectacle. Brown's spirited defence of pay policy won him a standing ovation from the bulk of the delegates. Cousins pointedly joined the TGWU delegation in the hall and sat, stony-faced, while the applause rang out. The cameras popped and flashed, the journalists' questions flowed. The government got the votes but was acutely embarrassed by Cousin's flagrant demonstration of dissent. It was a public rejection of the doctrine of Cabinet collective responsibility, a defiance which should have brought the sack. Not so. Wilson's determined priority was to hold the government and the party together, if humanly possible. That meant him compromising, holding back from a showdown.

Harold Wilson is a greatly underrated prime minister and Labour leader. To span Labour's warring factions, to negate the fratricide, to smother the outrageous irresponsibilities and absurdities that are an inherent part of the party's make-up, was an immeasurable achievement. Whether it was to the ultimate good of party and country is arguable. A less flexible approach would have been better for the long-term interests concerned. Wilson talked tough but his real penchant was for the mid-course, for pacification. It earned him a reputation for deviousness which was not entirely unjustified. The Left turned the inches he conceded to them into yards.

Yet Wilson survived the cauldron of Labour politics and brought the party from the despair of defeat in 1970 back to government again. It was under Wilson that Labour became established as a natural party of government, a bequest briefly enjoyed by his successor, Jim Callaghan, before it was squandered under the hapless leadership of Michael Foot.

Throughout 1965, Cousins simmered. There were frequent tales of resignation threats. He was reluctant to strike the final blow while Labour retained its slim-line Commons majority. Wilson worked furiously to keep him on board. It was simply a matter of time.

Wilson called the general election in March 1966. He gambled on increased electoral support. Labour swept back with a landslide majority of 96 and 47.9 per cent of the total poll. People accepted that Labour needed more time if it was to cope with the aftermath of Conservative misrule. However, the highly encouraging election result did nothing to ease the economic pressure. The incomes policy was tightened again.

Industrial troubles loomed, and in mid-May the seamen went on strike. Left-wingers made the running on the National Union of Seamen's Executive Committee and in its key port branches. They exploited longstanding and festering grievances, not only against the ship-owners but also against the NUS, passively led for many years by an old-style right-winger, Sir Tom Yates. Yates had gone and his successor, Bill Hogarth, a pleasant, easygoing man, was no match for the now entrenched and well-organized Left. Hogarth groped for a face-saving way out of the stoppage but the ship-owners were obdurate and cited government pay policy as legitimate evidence of the need to stand firm. Hogarth, squeezed between the employers and his own militants, had little room for manœuvre.

The government declared a state of emergency. The strike dragged on, crippling the ports, causing food shortages and threatening exports, jobs and the pound. Anxiety mounted, and the temperature shot up when Prime Minister Wilson told the Commons that the NUS was the victim of a Communist Party conspiracy and denounced the union's left-wingers as 'a tightly knit group of politically motivated men'. It was an over-simplification for the seamen's lot was not a happy one. The 'plotters' fomented trouble. It was part of their scheme to wrest control of the union. They ensured that there was no early settlement. But their intrigues would have failed if so many of the ordinary members had not felt thwarted and degraded enough to back the strike.

(One familiar figure among my reporting friends and contemporaries during the wearisome dispute was a burly, bluff, redheaded Yorkshireman, now Sir Bernard Ingham, then on the *Guardian* newspaper and later for many years Mrs Thatcher's controversial Press Secretary.)

Eventually, the TUC's George Woodcock persuaded the NUS Executive Committee to move towards a compromise. A committee of inquiry under Lord Pearson worked out a formula which paved the way to a settlement.

As the seamen's strike ended, Frank Cousins quit the government. It was a sledgehammer blow, but the only real surprise was that he had stuck it out for so long. His resignation letter made it plain that wages policy was the cause of his departure. He attacked it as 'fundamentally wrong'. He went on to lead Labour's Commons rebels against it and, resuming his TGWU and TUC roles, spearheaded the extra-parliamentary opposition to it as well.

George Brown, volatile as ever, was also on the brink of resignation. He was desperate for devaluation rather than the next round of cut and freeze agreed by the Cabinet majority. Brown did resign, but then withdrew his resignation. The 'July measures' crisis package went ahead, including a six-month freeze on price and wage rises to be followed by six months of 'severe restraint'. There were fines for any breach of the standstill. Brown soldiered on unhappily to pilot the necessary legislation through the Commons, but his heart was not in it.

A month later Brown became Foreign Secretary. The DEA never recovered from the loss of its buccaneering first boss. Brown's exasperating combination of bombast and drive, his unscholarly but perceptive economic and industrial know-how and his sheer force of personality, carried the DEA along – usually at a gallop. His bruised and battered staff recognized his talents, his commitment and the mental and physical strain he endured. They mostly gave him loyal protection and help, which says much for the man himself. Brown was succeeded at the DEA by Michael Stewart, grey, sombre and miscast.

Education was Stewart's forte, and Brown was a pretty impossible act to follow.

That autumn's TUC conference in Blackpool brought a harsh warning from Prime Minister Wilson of the risk of two million unemployed. He described the challenge ahead as 'the greatest, I believe, in our peacetime history'. He told the unions that they must co-operate. He collected his standing ovation – but not, of course, from the resentful Cousins and the TGWU delegation.

Woodcock was absent, the victim of a mild heart attack, and his deputy, Vic Feather, marshalled the TUC General Council's pro-government case with success. Cousins opposed and, in the course of his remarks, he spoke, not for the first time, of the need for 'social democracy' – in retrospect, a curious turn of phrase for such an avowed socialist, but unnoticed at the time. The conference voted by a slender margin to back the General Council and to 'reluctantly acquiesce' to the government's freeze.

TUC right-wingers were privately vitriolic about Cousins. Arch-critics like Sidney Greene, of the railwaymen, the rail clerks' Bill ('Willie the Wasp') Webber, the AEU's Bill Carron and Fred Hayday, of the General and Municipal Workers, believed that 'The Big Fella' indulged his outsized ego to betray the Labour government.

It was too glib an explanation. Cousins was indeed vain and egotistical. He was a gift to Tory newspapers, anxious to magnify every minor party difference, let alone the head-on conflict which he promoted. But Cousins was also a stubbornly principled and proud man. He told a left-wing Tribune fringe meeting at that year's Labour conference why he resigned from the government. 'A man is only as big as his integrity', he said. Cousins was neither vindictive nor a plotter. Other left-wingers, politicians and trade unionists, despaired of him as any kind of tactician. He put his head down and charged, more the rampaging rhinoceros than the customary TUC carthorse. His would-be allies could do little other than stumble after him. Cousins was wrong – on the Bomb, on pay policy, over his decision to join a government in which he was destined to be a misfit. The upside was his genuine enthusiasm for his Ministry of Technology role, despite his disheartening parliamentary experience, but resignation was more or less inevitable, since he was out of step on too many issues.

Cousins went on kicking furiously as the pay policy got tougher. A White Paper in November 1966 announced a nil norm for rises for the following year, with exceptions for the very low paid, or for genuine productivity. March 1967 brought yet another White Paper. The nil norm stayed, but the exemptions were extended and penalties were dropped. Woodcock helped to ease things by persuading a special TUC conference to endorse a tightening of the TUC's own wage vetting procedures.

Industrial unrest

Later in the year there was more serious industrial trouble. There were unofficial dock strikes which lasted for six weeks in both London and Liverpool. They were denounced by Ray Gunter, the Minister of Labour, as a Red plot. He used terms reminiscent of Wilson's condemnation of the seamen. Gunter claimed that the TGWU had lost control of its members and so it had. The remarks infuriated Cousins who had clashed frequently with Gunter within the Cabinet. It was one more aggravation for 'The Big Fella'.

Gunter, President of the Transport Salaried Staffs' Association, the rail clerks' union, was a stocky, florid-faced Welshman, and an outspoken right-winger. He was well qualified to identify plotters. He was mixed up in most of Labour's internal intrigues, including an abortive attempt to get rid of Wilson. He leaked information to selected journalists about the squabbles inside Labour's National Executive Committee. Gunter appointed Sir Jack Scamp to head an inquiry into the dock strike, and Scamp settled it. Sir Jack, GEC's Industrial Relations Director, was emerging as the nation's top industrial troubleshooter. He was straightforward, trusty and fully deserved his reputation on both sides of industry for objectivity and impartiality.

Another emerging industrial influence was Joe Gormley, then the Lancashire miners' leader. He began to play a major part on Labour's National Executive Committee. Gormley was wary of all the politicos. He offered the unvarnished view that since the unions grubstaked the party, they should control it. He was a determined adversary of the Executive's left-wingers – Tony Wedgwood Benn, Ian Mikardo and their ilk.

Gormley blamed his failure to become the National Union of Mineworkers' General Secretary in 1968 on his close involvement with Labour at national level. He reckoned that government wage restraint made Labour so unpopular with rank-and-file miners that they voted instead for his left-wing rival, Lawrence Daly. Gormley started as hot favourite, but Daly won the pithead ballot. Gormley had to wait until 1971 for national office – the NUM presidency.

His ballot-box experience was paralleled by that of the AEU's John Boyd. He too, was a right-wing member of Labour's ruling body and master-minded the AEU's anti-Communist internal organization. He confidently expected to succeed Lord Carron, the retiring president. Once again, the favourite fell. Hugh (now Lord) Scanlon was elected with support from the Communists and all those other left-wingers who ensured that the engineering union was in a state of perpetual election turmoil and instability – a situation that still prevails. It was like a wake in Carron's office at Peckham after the result was announced. Boyd, a Scot and a Salvation Army tuba player who nevertheless liked 'a wee sweet sherry', was a crestfallen figure. Carron shook his head wearily. 'It's a bad day for the union,' he said.

There was mounting industrial mayhem, a spate of unofficial strikes. The Conservative Opposition latched onto opinion polls that disclosed overwhelming public support for action against wild-cat stoppages. The Tories produced their own legislative proposals.

By now the TUC faltered in its backing for Woodcock's voluntary pay-vetting system. He won a narrow majority to carry on at another TUC conference of union executives, but it all looked increasingly fragile. Nor could it any longer satisfy a government under continued pressure from the so-called 'gnomes of Zurich', our international creditors. There were new measures to allow wage and price rises to be delayed for twelve months, for price cuts and for limits on rents and dividends.

George Brown had had enough. He resigned as Foreign Secretary. Wilson had to reshuffle his Cabinet pack. Sterling had at last been devalued. Roy Jenkins was Chancellor with the declared aim of 'a stiff Budget followed by two years of hard slog'. Callaghan was Home Secretary and Barbara Castle ousted Gunter at the renamed Department of Employment and Productivity, formerly the Labour Ministry. Castle, redheaded firebrand, was mistress of the calculated tantrum, tiresome but tireless. Callaghan, urbane, artful and dispassionate, was her *bête noire*. The two were worthy antagonists.

Gunter had called his Ministry a 'bed of nails' but he bitterly resented his enforced shift to the Ministry of Power – a downgrading. He had set up a Royal Commission on the unions and employers' organizations, under Lord Donovan. (He told me that he dearly wanted to be around to implement legislation arising from Donovan, and was disappointed that he would not see it through.) It was not long before Gunter, a longtime foe of Wilson, and soured by his treatment, quit the government.

The Donovan Report, published that same year, made many sound and some far-reaching proposals for the reform of industrial relations. They were lost in the uproar and convulsions over 'In Place of Strife', the most explosive of all the government's White Papers affecting the unions. That document, soon to make its appearance, was premeditated suicide. That, though, is wisdom with hindsight – an attribute which many politicians and commentators acquired on this most agonizing of all Labour's conflicts with the unions.

First though, Roy Jenkins introduced the most severe peacetime Budget ever. Tension with the unions grew, and government pay policy was finally overturned at both TUC and Labour Party 1968 autumn conferences. Sir Leslie Cannon, in a bravura performance, made a lone attempt to convince the TUC that incomes restraint was still essential in a planned economy. There was no support for this voice of moderation.

Inside Labour's pre-conference National Executive Committee, a rebellious Jim Callaghan joined forces with the government's critics from the unions, a warning of Cabinet dissension to come. On the conference floor there was a huge majority for Cousins's TGWU motion which called for the repeal of the prices and incomes laws and rejected any further legislation which 'would curtail basic trade union rights'.

It was time for Frank Cousins to hand over the reins at the TGWU. Harry Nicholas was now Labour's General Secretary and Jack Jones was a racing certainty to head the biggest union. There were rumblings of discontent. The union's bus section officials decided that Jones should be opposed. A pamphlet by the Union's Education Department head, Tony Corfield, called 'Collective Leadership in the TGWU', attacked 'the cult of personality' under Cousins and implied that this would continue under Jones. It was to no avail. Jones cantered to victory with a vast majority over three other candidates. Corfield later 'resigned'.

Industrial reform: Barbara Castle v. the unions

Those adverse decisions at the TUC and Labour conferences did nothing to dissuade Wilson and Barbara Castle of the need to act on the strike front. Their new contention was that anti-strike legislation could prove a deal more effective than prices and incomes policy. It would be more popular with the public and should pacify Britain's creditors, especially the International Monetary Fund.

New Year 1969 began with preliminary skirmishing as Castle outlined her plans to industry leaders. She wanted a 'cooling off' period before a strike was called, compulsory ballots for strikes against the national interest and an Industrial Relations Commission to investigate strikes and to be able to enforce its decisions. The Confederation of British Industry's Director General, John Davies, said that it was like 'taking a nutcracker to crack a cannonball'. (He told me that Mrs Castle was just blowing at the problem.)

The employers' view, expressed by Davies, later a Conservative Cabinet minister, was very different to that of the TUC. Cousins, still on the General Council until the next Congress in September, wanted Castle's package chucked out, lock, stock and barrel. He was overruled after Woodcock argued that parts of it were worth considering and could assist the unions. But even right-wingers vociferously opposed the 'cooling off' period and balloting proposals. In fact, Woodcock, though publicly cautious, was privately sympathetic to much that Castle sought. Within a couple of weeks of the talks opening, he was tipped as the likely Chairman of her Industrial Relations Commission, and rightly so.

On 18 January 1969, the 22,000-word White Paper, 'In Place of Strife', was published. The title was adapted from Aneurin Bevan's book *In Place of Fear*, but strife was built into the document. All the ideas which aroused TUC enmity were retained, along with many others of a more helpful nature, such as the right to belong to a union. Mrs Castle summed up: 'It reconciles the right to strike with the need to safeguard the rights of the community and protects the community from the senseless disruption of avoidable strikes.' Six months of fierce and bloody brawling were to elapse before, in effect, she was forced to eat her brave words. Serious industrial disorder bedevilled or threatened the car industry, the docks, steel and the airlines. One-day wild-cat strikes were planned in protest against the Castle blueprint, and the Left worked overtime against her. Workers reckoned that militancy paid. Unions won rises which were unjustified within the terms of the incomes policy, and the government turned a blind eye. The TUC's voluntary vetting system was less and less meaningful.

(I wrote in the *Daily Express* that it was tragic that 'just as the long-awaited breakthrough appears to have been won – encouraging trade and output figures, vastly improved industrial investment prospects, falling unemployment – Britain faces a fresh outbreak of its underlying industrial malaise.' Of Castle's plans, I said: 'She is justified in claiming that the bulk of her proposals would bolster official union leadership. Equally, there are justifiable misgivings among union chiefs of goodwill about the practicability of some of her ideas. Yet her strength remains the apparent inability of the unions to force the pace of change themselves.')

Mrs Castle, encouraged by Woodcock's privately friendly reaction, was convinced that she could bulldoze her proposals onto the Statute Book. Unfortunately for her, Woodcock had not read the prevailing mood of the TUC General Council – an indication of his frosty relations with so many of its members. It was a costly misjudgement. Moreover, Home Secretary Callaghan joined the union antagonists in a 16–5 vote against 'In Place of Strife' during angry exchanges on Labour's National Executive Committee. Fleet Street made the most of that fact, and Callaghan's relations with Wilson and Castle plunged to rock bottom.

There was a heated meeting with the TUC at Downing Street. Vic Feather was the TUC's Acting General Secretary, replacing Woodcock, now heading the newly established Industrial Relations Commission. Feather told Wilson that there was some pride in Britain not using the law in industrial relations compared with other countries. He added trenchantly: 'If you want German behaviour, you need German people.' Wilson hardly ranked with Bismarck, the Kaiser or Adolf Hitler, but the TUC was at war, and rhetoric was all part of the battle.

Wilson and Castle refused to budge. Then came the first concession in what was to turn into a rout. Castle dropped the proposal for compulsory ballots before strikes and sidestepped the prospect of jail for those who defied the new laws. But this was not enough for Feather and the recalcitrant TUC. Wilson, for his part, struggled to hold the line at a special all-day session of the Cabinet and the Party Executive at 10 Downing Street. He declared: 'Last time our slogan was "Government with guts". We are not going to be the government that loses its guts under pressure.'

Wilson and Feather shared a platform at the Post Office Workers' fiftieth anniversary jubilee rally at Bournemouth. The glimmer of a compromise began to appear. Or, more accurately, a glimmer of the government's ultimate capitulation. Wilson talked of the TUC producing an 'effective' alternative to the government's scheme. He even forecast that when the union celebrated its centenary 'every speaker on the platform will pay tribute to what Barbara has achieved by her legislation, and more widely, as the greatest charter of constitutional trade union advance in the whole history of Britain's industrial relations.' There was some booing at a claim that was extravagant then and now seems ridiculous but the jeers were swamped by the applause. Despite all the union anxieties and suspicions, Wilson received a standing ovation. It was, however, Feather's speech that triumphed. His message was simple – drop the sanctions and restore unity.

(I recall that conference too, for a typical, warmhearted Feather touch. The postmen's leader, Tom Jackson, invited journalists' wives to the rally since it was a celebratory occasion. It coincided with my wife Pat's birthday, something that must have been mentioned in bar-room chat. Feather, despite the immense pressure on him, slipped away to buy her a big box of chocolates.)

Next day, Wilson met the full TUC General Council at Downing Street. The TUC rubbed in the Donovan Commission's findings: 'that the criminal law should not be brought into the field of industrial relations'. The union team proposed instead a do-it-ourselves scheme to give the TUC more central authority to deal with unofficial strikes. It was enough to allow Wilson to promise to postpone legislation until after the TUC held an emergency conference in early June to ratify its own plan. Nevertheless, the key question remained: just what sanctions did individual unions have over their members and how often did they use them? It was a question that so far the TUC had declined to address.

There was growing opposition inside the Parliamentary Labour Party to the government's proposals. Trade union sponsored MPs were under pressure from their unions to resist legislation. Even Aubrey Jones, the PIB Chairman, chipped in to tell the government that it had got its priorities wrong. A prices and incomes policy, he said, was far more important to the control of inflation than the industrial relations package. More talks between Wilson, Castle and the TUC failed, however, to persuade the unions to accept the need for tougher discipline by the TUC over affiliated unions and by unions over their members.

By the eve of the TUC's special 6 June 1969 conference at Croydon – only the second of its kind in the TUC's hundred-year history – the big block votes were lined up behind the TUC's own plan and against the government. Only one big union differed, the ever-awkward electricians. They were critical of the inadequacy of the TUC's powers. The union's president, Sir Leslie Cannon, said that although the government had stimulated controversy 'far beyond the bounds of its economic importance', union 'backwoodsmen' were even more to blame.

Not for the first time, his was a lone voice of dissent. Vic Feather claimed that the unions 'are as conscious of the national interest as the government and much more so than most of our critics'. Speaker after speaker condemned the Castle ideas. Mrs Castle, anticipating the unpalatable outcome, responded even before the conference was over. She sent a chill letter by hand to Feather, again seeking guarantees from the TUC that its decisions would be complied with by individual unions and by strikers.

On 12 June Wilson agreed to drop the penal clauses from the legislation if the TUC tightened up its rules for dealing with unconstitutional strikes. But the TUC would shift no further. The union leaders sensed an all-out victory, which stiffened their resolve. The following day, further talks at Downing Street ended in failure, but Wilson and Castle hinted at a new approach to the vital question of sanctions. On 19 June Wilson caved in completely, and agreed to drop any trace of penal sanctions against unofficial strikers. It was a resounding success for the unions' fiercely sustained campaign. They had too many guns, too much firepower, for the government, which knew that it faced an horrendous revolt among its own MPs if it pressed on.

Failure of industrial reform: the 'solemn and binding' undertaking

Inside No.10, Wilson, Castle and Feather gave a joint press conference, all smiles and bonhomie. They spelled out the TUC's 'solemn and binding' undertaking that its new rules on unofficial strikes would be firmly implemented – rules which could lead to the expulsion from the TUC of a defiant union which failed to act against members in a wild-cat stoppage. Everyone put the best possible face on it but it was an humiliation for Wilson and an even greater one for Castle. Their cherished scheme had vanished on a TUC-created funeral pyre.

That July, in the Isle of Man, the TGWU's 800-strong delegate conference gave Frank Cousins an extraordinary send-off. There were six standing ovations for him during seventy-five minutes of fervent tributes. The delegates were out of their seats three times more to applaud his wife, Nance. It is doubtful if any trade union leader has ever had a more remarkable valedictory demonstration. (I asked Cousins what he saw as the milestones along his union road. He said: 'Milestones miss the point. Things happen through a lot of hard work, through a lot of little steps forward.')

The TUC's Portsmouth conference that September showed the familiar old carthorse once more lumbering along aimlessly. Feather, about to be confirmed as General Secretary, told me how much he wanted to get on with the job of modernizing the unions and their structures, and with tackling the vexed question of the TUC's future role. Instead, however, the battle lines with the government were redrawn, this time to force Wilson to scrap all sanctions to control wages. Some union leaders wanted incomes policy, already watered down to a weak and sorry mixture, to be abandoned altogether. Others thought that the PIB should be retained on a purely advisory basis.

Wilson delivered a direct and distinctly unwelcome message to the delegates: that continued wage restraint was vital and that there must be no backsliding on the binding undertaking over unofficial strikes. There was no standing ovation for him this time, and the conference went on to vote for the outright abolition of prices and incomes policy, and of the PIB. Cousins finally bowed out of the TUC with a characteristic parting shot. He said: 'If the political party wants to take advantage of the great strength we have, it should learn to lean on us, not to stand on us.'

It was all basically a reflection of the lingering resentment over the protracted anti-strike laws row. It reflected too, the desire for revenge on Barbara Castle by some of the TUC men who wanted to drive her from office. In the who-caused-what controversy, her critics believed that female fanaticism was the culprit. That was never more than a half-truth. It was Harold Wilson who first convinced himself that the Donovan Commission recommendations were wet and that the law was vital to industrial relations reform. Mrs Castle was the willing collaborator and architect of the detail. She can afford a wry smile as she views the wholesale and durable Thatcherite reforms of the eighties.

Any hopes that Cousins's departure would ease the government's problems with the unions were quickly dashed. The new left-wing alliance of his successor, Jack Jones, and the engineers' head, Hugh Scanlon, was destined to make life as difficult as ever for Wilson and the Labour leadership. It didn't take long. There were squalls at Labour's Brighton conference just a month after the TUC's defeat of the government. Jones was at the forefront of a confrontation over pay. For once, George Brown, the Deputy Leader, tried to play the peacemaker but Jones dismissed his bid as 'the usual dangerous waffle'.

By late October, pay policy was virtually a dead duck. Chancellor Roy Jenkins's fiscal policy was relied on to check wage inflation. Barbara Castle produced a new White Paper which contained the clear implication that union defiance on pay would mean higher unemployment. She warned: 'All those who exercise market power in the economy, whether in the fields of goods, services or labour, need to be accountable for their actions to the community at large.' It was vintage Barbara, with no trace of apology. She went further, slapping the unions down for not helping sufficiently to solve the plight of the low paid. She said that if every rise won by the low paid became a new 'floor' for automatic rises for the higher paid, it produced inflation, not social justice.

Early in 1970 Castle again changed course. She got Cabinet backing to merge the PIB and the Monopolies Commission into a new Commission for Industry and Manpower, to end existing powers to delay pay and price rises and to retain only a reserve power to get early warning of pending price, dividend and pay increases. Not surprisingly, it was the employers who now attacked, accusing Labour of contracting out on the pay front despite a spate of big pay demands.

The statutory lid was off and pay rises soared. Castle's 2.5–4.5 per cent norm was largely ignored, and the TUC scrapped its wage-vetting committee. Incomes policy, said Jack Jones, was now a 'dirty word'. The CBI told its members to stop notifying price rises.

Chancellor Jenkins warned that his Budget would be tapered to take account of the wages' explosion, but the stampede was on. London busmen got 16.5 per cent rises, dockers added 25 per cent to the port employers' annual pay bill, service men and women got up to 20 per cent and lorry drivers won an incredible 45 per cent award. Unions rejected as inadequate offers of 18 per cent for Ford workers and 19 per cent for seamen. The 1969 strike figures were revealed – 6,772,000 working days lost, the worst for a decade. Meanwhile, unemployment rose to nearly 630,000 – the highest for two years.

In May 1970 Barbara Castle finally got round to her Industrial Relations Bill, which was by now shorn of everything that might revive union hostility. The lion had become a mouse, and though it was now claimed that her original plan for sanctions was 'an important catalyst for reform', this was merely a platitude trotted out to try to obscure the harsh fact of failure.

The Tories in the ascendancy

A general election was imminent and a Harris Poll found that most people wanted a government that would take a tougher line with the unions. They meant a Tory government. That included a 2–1 majority of trade unionists. There were big opinion poll majorities in favour of secret ballots before strikes, for a 'cooling off' period and for legally binding agreements. The Tories had produced 'Fair Deal at Work', their plan for industrial relations reform. Their spokesman on labour affairs, Robert (now Lord) Carr, worked assiduously to get the case across. He talked privately to any union leader who would meet him. He advocated a positive set of rules, laying down rights and obligations for both unions and employers. Thus the Tories were set to capitalize on Labour's twin failure to control strikes and maintain a viable incomes policy.

Every post-war government has been compelled to concern itself with wage inflation but the bold Labour plan of 1964, seen as the keystone of the arch of economic growth, was at an end. It had not all been adverse. Most estimates allowed the policy a measurable restraining influence on pay rises of around 1 per cent a year. Price rises too, were checked. The PIB reports were often constructively damning in their disclosures of industrial waywardness and malpractice. But the policy was always too fragile to take the strain. 'In Place of Strife' struck the killer blow, removing the remnants of union support for anything that interfered with so-called free collective bargaining. Each time incomes policy foundered, it was intensified. The original idea was to exert strong restraint on the collective bargaining process by voluntary means and primarily by exhortation. Domestic economic chaos and the external pressure of the international bankers led to more and more statutory control. Avoidance – on a par with tax avoidance – became the name of the game. There were plenty of loopholes to exploit. The government, embattled over its strike laws, was unable to fight on two fronts. The pay policy rules were openly flouted with none of the punitive results which illegality invited. Group after group of workers cascaded through the crumbling dam.

Early on, the volunteers were there. Self-restraint became a temporary national pastime, and some workers agreed to postpone or reduce rises that were due. The policy was simple enough for all to understand. But once it was refined, once the jargon took over and White Papers flooded out, each producing some fresh complication and element of compulsion, so support dwindled.

44

The Tories were out to raise the temperature on industrial relations and especially on unofficial strikes and runaway union power. They knew their election winner. Their leader, Edward Heath, told a Tory trade unionists' conference in April 1970: 'The reform of industrial relations remains at the heart of our economic strategy. It will be the central plank of our election platform. It will be introduced in our first parliamentary session.' Heath attacked wild-cat strikes and restrictive practices – 'a stranglehold on industrial opportunity'. Labour, he asserted, allowed itself to be pushed over by the unions. In less than five and a half years of Labour government there were more strikes than in the previous thirteen years of Conservative government. Labour, he proclaimed, abdicated its responsibility.

Heath spelled out the extensive legislative programme which would provide 'the kind of shake-up industrial relations in Britain need'. There would be 'cooling off' periods and secret ballots before strikes which could endanger the national economy or the public interest. But there would be no penal clauses or fines on strikers, or jail for them. The remedy would be civil damages, with the unions (or employers) footing the bill, if at fault.

Prime Minister Wilson called an election in June 1970, in effect choosing a head-on confrontation with the Tories on industrial relations. He had little option. He berated Heath for irresponsibly endangering, for electoral purposes, 'the whole system of industrial relationships which wise men on both sides of industry have given their lives to building', and did his utmost to debunk the Tory case and 'sordid' record. He claimed that TUC intervention in more than 150 disputes since the Downing Street binding undertaking had saved an estimated two million man days for industry.

He may have rallied his own troops, but the public was unconvinced. Opinion polls suggested a clear-cut Labour victory, but, as it turned out, misled everyone. The voters decided that it was time for a change, and former Labour supporters simply stayed at home. The party's vote sank by nearly one million. Labour had 287 seats in the Commons, compared with 363 in 1966. Edward Heath was at Downing Street with a substantial overall parliamentary majority. (I had my personal prize as the newly elected Labour MP for Islington East but I would not be bolstering a new Labour government.)

Labour's overall record in government was far from disastrous. That inherited trade deficit of £800 million was turned into a £600 million surplus. Social legislation was impressive, including major

45

improvements in education, big rises for pensioners and the introduction of redundancy payments. But the union troubles overshadowed all this. Labour and the unions had left it too late to paper over the cracks and as a consequence both lost out.

4

Heath Humbled

Labour fought the 1970 general election free from most of the ideological baggage of the fifties, such as a sweeping nationalization shopping list, the overtones of Clause 4 and unilateral nuclear disarmament. In the post-election inquest it was entitled to reiterate, in its own defence, that the Wilson government grappled with that inherited balance of payments deficit of unsuspected enormity and turned it into a surplus. It did so despite the continuing traditional hostility of the international bankers and the ultimate non-cooperation of the trade unions.

But the potential impact of direct government intervention on economic management had been foolishly, if not recklessly, overstated. Expectations of a vigorous economic growth rate were dashed. Accordingly, resources were never available for the major expansion of public services and for the radical attack on poverty that was required if Labour objectives were to be realized.

No one could fairly accuse Wilson and his ministers of not striving to find the elusive answers to the age-old twin problems of labour relations and pay. There had been promising periods, but the end result was failure – a wet-shirt agreement which hid nothing and fooled nobody, least of all the participants. Labour could properly declare that the wages issue would not go away, that no government could evade it. (That remains the case today.) It could argue too, from bitter experience, that Britain's economic shortcomings and the sheer awfulness of its industrial structures made long-term voluntary constraint inconceivable in the foreseeable future – as Edward Heath was soon to discover. Whatever the underlying reasons, Labour's six years in office had produced no solutions, only a series of crises.

The new parliament met on 2 July 1970 to hear the Queen's Speech – the new Conservative government's legislative programme. Heath announced straightaway that an Industrial Relations Bill was top priority. Inevitably, the insensitive unions flouted the election result and helped Heath along. Before the month was out the government took emergency powers to deal with the first national dock strike since 1926, the start of a relentless string of industrial disputes that proved to be a salient feature of the Heath years.

The dock strike

The dock strike was something of a turning point for the TGWU leader, Jack Jones. Jones, tough, militant, left-wing, nevertheless struggled mightily to avoid a showdown, but was let down by the dockers. They accused him of a 'sell-out' and rejected out of hand his dramatic television appeal to work normally for another forty-eight hours to allow a delegate conference to consider a fresh offer on the part of the employers. Jones habitually pushed for industrial democracy but his passion for letting the activists decide caught up with him. He was justified in feeling disillusioned as the shop stewards made all the running.

The dockers' actions had a marked effect on Jones. He was never again the same uninhibited champion of the rank and file. He tried to lead from the front and instead of the display of trust and loyalty to which his record entitled him, those dockers gave him the bum's rush. From then on, he seemed to move steadily away from his syndicalist inclinations, and was soon to play a crucial role in the creation of the Social Contract, Labour's new economic lynchpin and a centralized concept far removed from any notion of workers' control.

The government set up an inquiry, headed by Lord Pearson, into the dock strike. His compromise proposals allowed both sides to get off the hook. But there were dire pay and industrial relations troubles ahead for Heath's Employment Secretary, Robert Carr.

Carr's Industrial Relations Bill

Heath was on the way to fulfil his pledge of statutory reform of industrial relations, but the unions volunteered nothing. They would have to be conscripted, as they would certainly not go cap-in-hand to 'consult' with Carr. Carr was prepared to discuss the details, but insisted that eight 'pillars', essential to the legal framework, could not be changed. Those 'pillars' included such all-important matters as the statutory right to belong or not to belong to a union, registration for unions, the presumption that collective agreements would be legally binding unless one side contracted out and the selective enforceability of procedure agreements. Any self-respecting shop steward, told by management that consultation would be so restricted as to be near meaningless, would create difficulties. The TUC gave the government the brush-off.

Carr's formal document was not available at the TUC's autumn conference, but the main proposals were known. They stemmed from 'Fair Deal at Work', the Tories' pre-election prospectus. Even so, the TUC conference was a dull affair. There was anti-government unity, but the demonstration of togetherness swirled over and blurred fundamental issues, such as wages and the plight of the low paid.

Labour's conference, a month later, was livelier. Roy Jenkins, in his first speech to delegates since taking over as the party's deputy leader, went down on a vote on incomes policy, but convincingly won the argument. He said that the whole conference knew 'in its heart' that Labour must produce a policy to control inflation if it was once more to offer itself as a credible governing party. (His speech bears repetition in the nineties.)

Britain was galloping into an inflationary mess as Heath's pre-election promise of direct action to reduce prices remained unfulfilled. Rather, government action had promoted price inflation, reflected, in turn, in pay demands. High wage settlements were bound to add to the prices–wages spiral. The dustmen were pacesetters following a 'dirty jobs' strike and an independent committee of inquiry under Sir Jack Scamp. Carr nobbled conciliation to prevent an improved employers' offer, but was left looking silly when the employers first raised the offer themselves, then accepted the further increase recommended by Scamp.

Carr reacted petulantly to the Scamp findings which did no more than acknowledge the economic and industrial facts of life, and dared to point out that there was no kind of incomes policy yardstick with which to measure the national interest. Scamp, a man of no political affiliation, was subjected to sustained and deliberate Tory denigration. He was their necessary scapegoat.

The pay cauldron bubbled ominously. The next test was likely to be with the health service ancillary workers, as their unions wanted them to get the same as the dustmen. Similarly, the miners, railwaymen and postmen were all lining up for big rises. The electricity and motor industries faced formidable union demands, and the building workers were restive.

Labour's problem was how to appear to be other than just bloody-minded in opposing the government's pay stance and more especially Carr's proposed measures for industrial relations. Barbara Castle's presence on Labour's Front Bench hardly helped, and Carr did his best to exploit her obvious handicap – the 'In Place of Strife' débâcle. Carr also made an absurd attempt to equate what the government sought with the Donovan Royal Commission proposals. So did Sir Geoffrey Howe, the Solicitor-General and the chief architect of 'Fair Deal at Work'. Carr used carefully selected quotations from Donovan, but the incompatibility between that report and his own plans was glaring.

Carr presented his 150-clause Industrial Relations Bill to parliament on 1 December 1970. Heath and his Cabinet wanted a blunderbuss with which to gun down the unions, and this was it. There were no surprises, scant deviation to meet the views of the critics. The TUC was able to claim that its boycott was well justified, that this was a government that would not listen. Carr's declared aim was to create an atmosphere in which strikes were a weapon of last, not first, resort. He got his legislation onto the statute book, but was unable to achieve the atmosphere he sought. The strikes rolled on.

Most TUC leaders backed the position of the engineers' Hugh Scanlon who said that the TUC should harness all affiliated unions 'in utmost opposition to the proposals before they become law'. The electricians' Sir Leslie Cannon again went out on a limb. He dismissed as nonsense the claim that the legislation would seriously undermine union power and authority or that it was an unwarranted interference in collective bargaining. The government received a mandate from the electors, he said, and the TUC should seek to change unsatisfactory features in the proposals by submitting reasoned amendments.

The electricity workers were on a go-slow and work to rule. Another state of emergency was declared. There were blackouts, inconveniences, hardships. Chancellor Anthony Barber accused the unions of 'blackmail'. There was a public backlash of hostility against the electricity workers and their union leaders, in particular Frank Chapple, who took over as chief negotiator from Cannon, who was by this time a very sick man. (I was in touch with Chapple who told me heatedly that Jim Callaghan asked him to call off the action because it was embarrassing Labour's Shadow Cabinet. He said that he told Jim where to put his request.)

The government set up a court of inquiry, under Lord Wilberforce. Chapple, resentful of political interference in an industrial dispute, did call off the action 'as an act of faith', despite union dissatisfaction with the court's terms of reference. The unions disliked the government's insistence that the court must consider 'the public and national interest' – an indication that Heath was edging towards criteria by which pay claims might be judged, despite the Tory condemnation of Scamp on this point. There was some heavy-handed advice to the court by John Davies, the former CBI chief who was now the Trade and Industry Secretary. He condemned as inflationary the 10 per cent offer by the employers, the Electricity Council – a comment which angered the unions who wanted far more.

It was rare for any governing party to lose its popularity so rapidly as the Conservatives did under Heath. By the end of 1970, the opinion polls showed a clear trend back to Labour. The Industrial Relations Bill was the government's best prospect of throwing up a smokescreen behind which other unpalatable Tory policies could be partially obscured, not least the inability to deliver the promised price cuts. Their strategy was to highlight union irresponsibility for trying to stop reforms which would get rid of strikes, especially the wild-cat variety.

Willie (now Lord) Whitelaw was Leader of the Commons. He liked to give the impression that he was out of his depth once technicalities entered into things. That way, he appeared to reason, astute journalists would see through his ploy and inform their readers that Willie was not as dumb as he looked and acted. It was quite clever – since he frequently did flounder out of his depth.

However, his tactics could not be faulted on the Industrial Relations Bill. He announced that it would be taken in all its stages on the floor of the Commons. Labour could hardly object to this full frontal exposure. They would have preferred to see this populist measure buried away in a Commons committee room for as long as possible. Now the Bill would be a major set-piece parliamentary engagement and could be presented by the government as the potential saviour of Britain's economic difficulties.

Prime Minister Heath was quick to capitalize on this. He used the Commons to praise 'the courage and determination of the British people' during the electricity dispute, and then implied that, had it been law, the Bill might have resolved the matter. In practice, few employers believed that the legislation's impact on industrial relations would match the government's dramatic predictions. The more informed view was that employers would tend to refrain from court action in disputes with their employees, rather than severely embitter shopfloor relations.

Heath, Carr and Co. were helped in their bluff by a compliant Labour Party. Wilson, Callaghan, Jenkins, and other perceptive members of the parliamentary leadership, privately shared the employers' view of the likely effects. Unfortunately, Labour was forced to play to the union and left-wing gallery, and they chose to unite the Labour movement by denouncing the Bill as coercive and blatantly anti-union.

The Bill was badly flawed, but Labour MPs overreached themselves in a way that could only benefit the government. Ministers knew that there was no more popular sport with the public than a spot of union-bashing, and Labour's defence of the indefensible spelled a valuable political bounty for Heath.

The government guillotined the Bill – limited its Commons debating time – which produced a noisy organized stunt in the chamber by left-wing Labour MPs. They crowded around the mace and the Speaker had to suspend the sitting. Some of the new intake of Labour MPs thought that this kind of private enterprise demonstration was stupidly counter-productive and damaged the party's credibility. There was a wide-spread public view of the Commons as a sort of asylum where too many of the inmates were senile and acted juvenile. (I sent off a protest letter on behalf of eight new MPs to the Parliamentary Labour Party's veteran Chairman, Douglas (now Lord) Houghton.)

But Labour's foibles were nothing compared to those of the government. It stumbled from one industrial crisis to the next. Wilberforce had yet to report on the electricity workers' pay, but there were strikes in the Post Office and at Ford. When Wilberforce pronounced, he recommended a slight increase in the employer's offer and his package, including the introduction of incentive bonus schemes, led to a settlement. If the original offer was inflationary – as ministers branded it – then this deal was inflation plus some. The government could only grin and bear it.

Labour's fragile unity cracked again. The Common Market brought renewed and frantic controversy as Heath pressed ahead for Britain's entry. The former Labour Cabinet minister Richard Crossman danced an extraordinary fandango to try to prove that the Labour Cabinet of which he was a member made no collective decision of support for joining the Common Market 'in principle'. He suggested that the

Wilson government only applied to test the price of entry. Crossman's intellectual gymnastics were an attempt to dissociate himself from that earlier Cabinet decision. He was rather like Macavity, T. S. Eliot's mystery cat:

> He always had an alibi and one or two to spare:
> At whatever time the deed took place – Macavity wasn't there.

And neither was Crossman.

(Wedgwood Benn is the latterday Macavity. Anyone hearing Benn's caustic criticisms of Labour in office must find it hard to believe that he was a Cabinet minister in every Labour Government after 1964.)

The truncated Industrial Relations Bill was through its Commons stages. There were 147 divisions. Labour MPs trooped through the voting lobbies throughout the evenings and the small hours of the mornings, sometimes until dawn, in a display of solidarity with the unions. Or, more accurately, of penitence over 'In Place of Strife'. It was tiring and futile. We stifled our misgivings, as we had to be seen by the unions to demonstrate for them. Privately, union leaders told me how little they cared about our antics. Publicly, they urged us on rather than upset their militants. This was lobby fodder at its most inedible.

Chancellor Barber introduced what *The Times* called the most purely Conservative Budget that the most senior of Mr Heath's rank and file in the Commons could remember. The Industrial Relations Bill closed Labour's ranks and, along with Tory wages policy, caused the more forward-looking union leaders to think again about a voluntary incomes policy for the long term. There was increasing recognition that Labour must offer a coherent incomes policy as part of its broad economic blueprint. There had to be a *quid pro quo* on the social front, and there were signs that Jack Jones, for instance, was thinking this way. The first glimmer was emerging of the Social Contract that was to be agreed between the unions and the next Labour government.

Meanwhile, a disillusioned George Woodcock quit as Chairman of the Commission for Industrial Relations, an institution boycotted by the TUC because of the Bill. Woodcock was replaced by Len (later Sir Len) Neal, British Rail's industrial relations chief. Neal, lay preacher, one-time Smithfield meat porter and ex-TGWU official, earned considerable respect from both sides of industry while at British Rail. I talked to him about his daunting new task and he said: 'When the emotion and anger over the Bill has subsided I hope that the unions will see that the CIR is a vehicle which can help them to operate more effectively within a new set of guidelines and that they have nothing to fear from it.' He was something of an optimist.

The TUC conference in Blackpool that autumn was mightily confused when it debated the new laws. The engineers' Hugh Scanlon successfully moved a motion which instructed unions not to register under the new Industrial Relations Act and to remove themselves from the provisional register, then in place. Scanlon was loudly cheered when he declared: 'If we are to ask the next Labour government to repeal this Act as a first priority, we have to say that we will pledge to the hilt that not one union will co-operate under the Act or participate in it.' It was to prove a sadly divisive decision which resulted in the subsequent expulsion from the TUC of a number of its affiliates.

(Scanlon was still in his militant phase, more concerned to parade his left-wing credentials than to offer a reasonable compromise to avoid domestic devastation among the unions. Like so many entrenched left-wingers, the good life eventually got to him and he mellowed. His often humorous company was preferable to that of his right-wing predecessor, Bill Carron, who could be a touch sanctimonious.)

By January 1972 there were one million people registered as unemployed. It was the first time in a generation that such a total had been reached. *The Times* called it 'a shocking occurrence in contemporary Britain'. Robert Carr favoured a voluntary incomes policy to help cut the jobless figure, and said: 'This Government wishes to do business with the TUC.' The chance of a deal was negligible so soon after the industrial relations legislation and while prices and rents soared.

(There were signs that Margaret Thatcher, the Education Secretary, was at odds with Prime Minister Heath. There was a public outcry against her but she couldn't be sacked. That would have been an admission by Heath that he had made a bad appointment – and he needed to retain a woman in his Cabinet. Had he got rid of her then, the politics of the eighties might have been very different, and 'Thatcherism' might never have become part of our day-to-day vocabulary. Perhaps no-one has been more conscious of this than the embittered Edward Heath.)

The miners' strike: victory for Gormley

The pay scene looked ugly again. The miners' union imposed an overtime ban in protest at a 7 per cent pay offer. The National Union of

Mineworkers went ahead with the first national pit strike in its history. The union, led by the astute Joe Gormley, had its ballot vote majority and did not bother to picket the pits. There would be no strike-breaking there. Instead, the union deployed men at the power stations, ports and coal depots, so stopping the movement of coal. The TUC called on other unions not to cross the picket lines 'in any circumstances'.

Arthur Scargill, then a relatively unknown NUM area official from Yorkshire, organized a highly successful mass picket at the Saltley Coke Depot, near Birmingham, – the largest coke depot in the country. The large-scale secondary picketing, intimidation and violence, was a new and brutish phenomenon in British industrial relations, and a foretaste of Scargill's tactics more than a decade later – tactics which brought ruinous defeat and decimation to his union and ensured punitive legislation.

Coal supplies dwindled and the government declared the now familiar state of emergency. A court of inquiry, under Lord Wilberforce, was not in time to prevent a three-day week for industry and massive power cuts, including big reductions in domestic usage of electricity. Wilberforce's findings conceded the bulk of the NUM case and led to a settlement, though the final deal which Gormley extracted from the Coal Board, with government approval, was far better than Wilberforce's recommendation. It had taken a six-week strike to achieve the deal, and it left Heath in a sorry mess.

Heath appealed to the unions to find a 'more sensible way' of dealing with pay problems. He sidestepped my Commons demand for a categorical assurance that he would not introduce a statutory wages policy, insisting instead on the importance of pending talks, under Neddy auspices, between the government, the CBI and the TUC, aimed at achieving voluntary agreement.

Those talks marked another shift in the tortuous government–union relationship. The TUC was deeply divided over the registration issue. Most unions were determined to retain their independence from the registrar's powers over their rule books and standards – a position owing more to emotion than to logic. But some unions felt obliged to register to avoid financial disadvantages.

The miners' victory changed attitudes. It was the first real indication that this government could be beaten. A renewed TUC unity took shape. Vic Feather was able to claim that the unions looked more closely towards the TUC for a lead and 'do not regard Congress House as being in an ivory tower'. Moreover, the revival of union spirit forced Heath towards the unthinkable – a form of incomes policy. Hence his enthusiasm for tripartite talks.

Heath received another hammer blow when a complex series of events in the docks brought a clash between the employers and the TGWU. Sir John Donaldson, the right-wing judge, headed the National Industrial Relations Court, another Industrial Relations Act product, and seen by the unions as an arm of Heath's government. Donaldson jailed five dockers for refusing to obey a court order to call off industrial action. Thousands went on strike, and not only in the docks. Britain was in chaos, until, after five days, the so-called Pentonville Five were freed through a cobbled-up legal wangle. Now unions like the electricians and the shopworkers, appalled by the imprisonments, voted to deregister. The unions were coming together again. The Industrial Relations Act was emasculated and on its way out.

Labour still had few answers of its own. The political editor of the *News of the World*, the late Anthony Shrimsley, reported on a 'small self-appointed team that is trying to produce a workable incomes policy'. (I had got together six of the 1970 intake of Labour MPs. They included Neil Kinnock, Michael Meacher and John Horam, who later moved to the SDP and then to the Tories.) Shrimsley rapped Labour's National Executive Committee for its latest 'rose-tinted' policy statement, adding: 'After the waffle of the original document, it is reassuring to know that some people at least are getting down to cases.'

The government now faced an economic nightmare. Unemployment during the summer of 1972 was more than 900,000, and winter promised one million plus, another post-war record for the taking. Inflation accelerated, an unusual happening when unemployment was high. Government-induced measures – Common Market entry, Value Added Tax and 'fair rents' legislation – pushed up living costs, which were in turn reflected in wage demands. The government–CBI–TUC talks ploughed on. There was no agreement, which was hardly surprising given the hidebound Heath in the chair and Jack Jones and Hugh Scanlon as the principal union figures.

The TUC's Brighton conference voted overwhelmingly that thirty-two unions which still defied TUC instructions by failing to deregister should be suspended from membership. Vic Feather told the miscreants that they should not forget their obligations to the TUC, but it was one of his least convincing performances. (It was clear to me, from a chat with him, that his heart wasn't in it.)

Moderate union leaders were privately convinced that the TUC's policy was stupid, especially on registration and on an instruction to boycott not only the National Industrial Relations Court and the Commission for Industrial Relations, but also all industrial tribunals. The tribunals went ahead with their necessary work. They dealt with unfair dismissal cases for aggrieved workers who now had no union representative on the tribunals nor alongside them at the hearings. It was a ridiculous situation and all the more absurd now that the detested Act was effectively neutered.

The TGWU's Jack Jones moved a crucial motion which rejected any form of wage restraint and instructed the TUC leaders to refuse any discussions with the government or the CBI which had this objective. The motion was carried unanimously.

One of the most-quoted speeches of the week was by the electricians' Frank Chapple. He was twice shut out of debates on industrial relations. Feather, the canny old 'fixer', knew that Chapple could be explosive and he wanted to keep the conference temperature down. He saw to it that Chapple was not called to the rostrum. It was a counter-productive move. The infuriated electricians' delegation walked out on the conference, and Chapple released to the press the speech that the TUC could not hear. It got widespread media coverage, far more than if he had been permitted to make it at the conference. Chapple said that the TUC's policy towards the Industrial Relations Act was a mistake from the start. The unions should have made use of the legislation where they could and should seek to change what was damaging. His stated view of the TUC: 'I don't know how the government sees you but, by God, you frighten me.'

It was Chapple at his most provocative. What was really galling for the TUC was that most of them knew that he was right but didn't dare to say so.

Behind the scenes: Wilson and the media

I was called to see Harold Wilson just before Christmas 1972. He asked me to speak from Labour's Front Bench on media matters. It was a swift leg up after only two and a half years in the Commons. Harold's ploy was that I should 'freelance' from the Front Bench, picking up any chance to harass the government on broadcasting or the press, areas where Heath was often clumsy and vulnerable. Wilson indicated that I would have ready access to him, without formality – a necessity in dealing with the fast-moving media scene. He suggested too, that my new job would lead to a major post in the next Labour government, with full responsibility for broadcasting and for government information services. My parliamentary life promised to be much enlivened.

There were some curious side effects when the appointment was announced, early in 1973. Tony Wedgwood Benn had sought my advice on union issues. Now he clearly wanted no more contact. His relations with Wilson were perpetually strained and it was as though I had joined the enemy camp – probably about the truth of it.

Neil Kinnock was another who became somewhat distant. He saw his way upwards as via his left-wing friends; saw himself even then as a prospective leader of the Left to follow the ageing Michael Foot. Neil was not going to compromise his long-term plan by any noticeable alignment with the current party leadership, however indirect. He stuck to that position throughout the years of Wilson–Callaghan government, and it paid off for him in the end. He became hail-fellow-well-met again when he sought election to the Shadow Cabinet in the wake of Labour's 1979 election defeat. It was back to 'How are you, kiddo?' (Still, Kinnock is likeable. He is also emotional, unstuffy, humorous, gutsy and with more intelligence than he gets credit for. But unstoppably voluble. Whether he is genuine prime ministerial material is arguable.)

Nor did I get the friendliest reception from Joe Haines, the former *Daily Herald* journalist who was now Wilson's Press Secretary. He had lorded it in media matters, and I was an unwelcome intruder, someone whose Fleet Street background was then rather more substantial than his own and also an elected politician. Haines was a good professional, but he was generally unpopular among the political reporters and conveyed a positive distrust of all journalists. He fed Wilson's paranoia about the media. There were times when his attitude was well justified but overall it did more harm than good. That paranoia ran right through Wilson's famous 'Kitchen Cabinet', but Marcia Williams, now Lady Falkender, was a friendly and helpful contrast to Haines. Wilson was buffeted by her tantrums but she could be a shrewd adviser and her loyalty to him was unquestionable.

Labour's National Executive Committee set up a communications group to produce reforms for the media. The hyperactive Mr Benn was the Chairman and I was a member. Labour was already committed to a full-scale inquiry into broadcasting, but newspapers posed a far more intractable problem. When speakers at Labour movement conferences want an easy round of applause, they need only to attack the 'capitalist press'. The much-peddled notion that newspapers are in some grand conspiracy to do down Labour is a nonsense. It still persists. The truth is less sinister. Since most newspapers are owned by Tory supporters, they lean heavily in that direction without the necessity for any organized plot.

Labour's death-wish has, over the years, given its predatory under-takers of the national press an easy quarry. There was, and is, a good deal of warranted concern over political balance throughout the media, but it is easier recognized than remedied, most suggested cures being worse than the disease itself.

Prices and incomes: Heath's about-turn

Back at Westminster, statutory wage control was in again. The Conservative Party's 1970 election-winning manifesto had been categorical: 'We utterly reject the philosophy of compulsory wage restraint.' It was a dangerous hostage to fortune. No wonder people see politicians as liars. Here was a fundamental principle, spelled out with intense clarity, now jettisoned like some piece of excess baggage. Heath implemented a three-month freeze on pay and prices – Phase One of a government incomes policy that was to continue from that time (November 1972), with variations, until the next general election.

In mid-January 1973 Heath unfurled the next stage of his anti-inflation plans. The *Sun* newspaper, not then on the rampaging Right, ran an editorial which was headed: 'Forget the party line.' It went on to declare: 'It is not the Tories who need a wages–prices policy and it is not Labour. It is all of us. . . . Today a Labour MP, John Grant, states boldly in the *Sun* why he is in favour of a prices and incomes policy.' The newspaper endorsed my argument that Labour must produce a viable alternative to Heath's proposals.

Heath announced that the government would allow increases of 4 per cent of the current pay bill, plus £1. He was moving up the incomes policy road which he had previously denounced. He stole more and more of Labour's clothes. His Counter-Inflation Bill, to bring in the second phase of his policy, got through its Commons second reading with a thirty-six vote majority.

By mid-February another pay crisis threatened. Gas workers and civil servants were in the vanguard of industrial action, and car workers, hospital workers and locomen looked sure to follow.

One-day strike

The TUC held a special conference in London which overwhelmingly backed a scatter-brained proposal for a one-day general strike. But unions were only 'invited' to join in. It was a typical TUC cock-up. Senior General Council members were dismayed at the decision and were worried that there would be an humiliatingly poor response from their members. That would be a bonus for the government. Meanwhile, those industrial troubles mounted. The striking gas workers were joined by London teachers and hospital ancillary workers. The locomen had a one-day stoppage.

Roy Jenkins made a speech in Oxford, dismissing the idea of a third political force, a new centre party, as 'profoundly unattractive'. He sharply criticized Labour for 'a slide to weakness' but said that the most likely result of a third force would be 'chaos on the Left and several decades of Conservative hegemony'. It turned into a self-fulfilling prophecy.

Wilson began to recapture much of his old verve and skill at the Commons despatch box. He made some telling speeches and his questions to Heath had more of that wit, bite and wicked humour which so distinguished him in his earlier days as Labour Leader. Heath became more testy and insecure as the pressure built up over pay and prices. Mortgage interest rates rose to 10 per cent, in contrast to the Tory election promise to make home-ownership easier. The government doled out a subsidy to the building societies to keep the increase down to 1 per cent.

Labour received a boost to morale when it won the 1973 GLC election, with fifty-eight seats to the Tories' thirty-two and two for the Liberals. (I had a key role in drafting the manifesto 'A Socialist Strategy for London' and wrote most of the election address which dropped through the letterboxes of every London elector. My contribution to the GLC victory was unexpectedly acknowledged by Harold Wilson who asked me to start work on drafting the party's manifesto for the next general election. Wilson did not trust the senior figures at Transport House, the party's headquarters, to do the job to his satisfaction. He was in perpetual conflict with them and was always on edge in his relationship with Labour's National Executive Committee. However, I persuaded Wilson that a one-man, secretly written manifesto was not a good idea.)

The TUC duly held its twenty-four-hour protest strike on May Day.

It was something of a non-event. Heath scorned these blundering artisans, claiming that 85 per cent of trade unionists stayed at work. He was not far wrong.

Heath in trouble

Elsewhere Heath was in trouble. Chancellor Anthony Barber announced a £600 million package of public spending cuts. Lord Lambton, Under-Secretary of State for the RAF, suddenly resigned for 'personal and health' reasons, but this turned out to be the result of a call-girl scandal. A couple of days later, Lord Jellicoe, Lord Privy Seal and Leader of the Lords, quit the government on similar grounds.

In the midst of all these government difficulties, Labour scored its usual spectacular own goal. The National Executive Committee voted to commit a Labour government to nationalize twenty-five of Britain's biggest companies. Wilson was furious and issued a statement to make it clear that the Shadow Cabinet would veto the plan's inclusion in Labour's general election manifesto. But that did not stop the gleeful diversion of media attention from Tory trauma to Labour's.

Heath got his Phase Two pay policy through its parliamentary stages. He ruthlessly hijacked past Labour policy, and his pay limit was a near repeat of the previous Labour government's norm. There was to be a continuing price freeze, except on fresh food, coal, steel and imports. There would be an 'early warning' system, first introduced by Labour in 1967. All this would be policed by a Price Commission and a Pay Board, copied from Labour's Prices and Incomes Board which Heath swept away disdainfully in 1970. Pay strikes could mean fines.

Heath presided in as big a rise in prices in three years as in the six years of Labour government before him. Since he took over, the average cost of a new house had nearly doubled and council rents had risen faster than ever before. Those out of work each month averaged nearly half as many again as under Labour, and twice as many days off were lost through industrial action.

This was no black propaganda, but rather the factual background against which Heath was anxious to talk to the TUC about Phase Three of his pay policy. The CBI's Director-General, Campbell Adamson, warned against a return to free collective bargaining because weaknesses in the system 'have directly led this country to a situation over the past years where increases in productivity have been exceeded two or three times by increases in earnings'. The TUC view was very different. The TUC's six-man team which met the government put the blame squarely on price rises. Jack Jones urged a return to free collective bargaining and Hugh Scanlon called the price curbs 'an empty charade'.

The scene was set for a showdown over pay and industrial relations. The miners shaped up ominously. Mick McGahey, the NUM's Communist vice-president, persuaded the union's annual conference to go for rises of £8 to £13 a week, and coupled this with a declaration that 'it is not negotiation in Downing Street but it is agitation in the streets of this country to remove this government that is required'. That was no help to the miners' cause, and I was among Labour MPs who signed a parliamentary motion reproving McGahey. His view was abhorrent too to the NUM President, Joe Gormley.

Gormley accepted an invitation from Heath to meet privately at Downing Street. Heath said that the miners were vital to the third stage of pay restraint which he must have. Gormley told him that there was no prospect of the miners knuckling down to a norm. They would have to have something on the top. Out of these discussions came an informal understanding – or so Gormley believed – that special payments for unsocial hours put in by the many miners on shift work could be the way out. It looked as though an uneasy compromise was hatched, but it was not to be.

The TUC teetered on the brink of withdrawal from talks with the government on voluntary pay restraint. Once the union leaders got details of the new Phase Three proposals – maximum rises of 7 per cent or £2.25 weekly – they rejected them. The talks broke down. The TUC declined to help the government to operate any statutory policy.

The miners threw out the Coal Board's 13 per cent offer of £2.25–£2.50 a week for them in cash terms. They sought a formal meeting with Heath to urge him to make them a 'special case' within Phase Three. This he refused to do. To Gormley's surprise and chagrin, Heath included unsocial hours among the items that justified above-the-norm payments rather than hold them back as a bargaining counter, a negotiable concession which might have headed off conflict. It was manifest ineptitude. The NUM imposed an overtime ban. That coincided with the Arab–Israeli Yom Kippur war which, in turn, brought a huge rise in oil prices and a 25 per cent reduction in oil supplies from the Arab states to the West. Heath declared yet another state of emergency, and had more abortive talks with the NUM. Maurice Macmillan, a hapless Employment Secretary, was replaced by

Willie Whitelaw, but the crisis worsened. To counteract it, Heath introduced a three-day working week. Floodlights were banned, street lighting was reduced and television shut down at 10.30 p.m.

(Harold Wilson decided that the industrial furore merited an increase in the size of Labour's Front Bench employment team. He asked me to add to my media responsibilities by also acting as one of two deputies to Reg Prentice, the employment spokesman.)

Len Murray, Vic Feather's successor as TUC General Secretary, showed some rare initiative. He tried to break the deadlock between the government and the miners, promising that if the government recognized the miners' 'exceptional situation' and settled with them, other unions would not use the settlement as an argument in their own pay negotiations. This was a major concession by the TUC, however belated, but for Heath acceptance meant the kind of retreat that did not figure in his bible of dogmatic leadership. It smacked of Labour's appeasement over 'In Place of Strife'. He should have grabbed the gift-wrapped compromise, but pride, stubbornness, arrogance or crass misjudgement prevented him from doing so. A Pay Board report offered a formula for making groups of workers into special cases within the terms of counter-inflation policy. That too, got short shrift from the government. The turndown of assistance from such a reputable source was even more inexplicable.

The miners balloted for an all-out strike. Everything pointed to a general election. The overriding issue being, 'Who governs?' The elected government or the unions? That was Heath's inevitable theme. He announced on 7 February 1974, that the election would be on 28 February.

Panic set in among Tory MPs, who flapped around like demented chickens. Morale was low, and some promising political careers were on the line. On the eve of his election announcement, Heath added substantially to the instability in his ranks. He disclosed that he had asked the Pay Board to deal with the miners' claim, using the special formula in the report which he had previously spurned. His turnabout went further. He promised that a new Conservative government would backdate any award by the Pay Board to 1 March.

Harold Wilson made great play with this remarkable capitulation. 'For the first time in history', he told television viewers, 'we have a general leading his troops into battle with the deliberate aim of giving in if they win.' In the Commons, the last parliamentary session prior to the election found MPs jamming the seats and gangways. Labour members chanted 'Goodbye' as ministers arrived. It was pantomime, but we really did feel that change was in the air.

None of this was enough for the miners. The union's leadership voted to keep the strike going, despite the election campaign. It was not the most helpful decision for Labour. Joe Gormley wanted the strike suspended. He pointed out that Heath's climbdown meant that the union had effectively won the battle. But he failed to carry his colleagues on this occasion.

Nor was the union enraptured by Harold Wilson. Earlier in the dispute, he pinched an idea put by Gormley to the Coal Board for extra payments to miners for time spent waiting and washing before and after shifts. It might have brought agreement but Gormley gave Wilson a confidential briefing on what was afoot. A cockahoop Wilson aired the proposal in the Commons as though it was his own idea. That ensured its rejection by the government – to Gormley's fury. (Gormley was never a Wilson fan and now reckoned that his judgement was fully justified.)

(I was with Harold Wilson in his Commons room during the pre-election period when news came through that the locomen were set for industrial action. Labour's union links always made the party vulnerable when strikes took place. Even the miners were a dubious political asset. A rail strike could lose Labour a bagful of votes, especially in the London commuter belt where a breakthrough was essential if we were to win the election. Wilson asked me to ring Ray Buckton, leader of the Association of Locomotive Engineers and Firemen (ASLEF). Buckton would be urged to suspend any action.

I got straight through to Buckton on the direct line to his Hampstead office desk. He said that his Executive Committee members, who decided on the stoppage, were packing their bags and were about to leave London for their homes around the country. He doubted if he could stop them or reassemble them again before the following week. I put Wilson on the line to him to impress upon him first-hand the importance of a stay of action. Buckton did manage to persuade his Executive members to hang on in London overnight. Next morning, they saw Wilson at the Commons, and soon after that, ASLEF's threatened strike was shelved, much to Labour's relief.)

A week before the election, the Pay Board announced that the miners should get 8 per cent more to bring them into line with manufacturing industry. This recommended cascade of money wrecked the government–Coal Board claim that the miners were already well above

64

the average in the earnings league and implied that the strike need never have happened if the government had done its homework. There was a fierce statistical wrangle over the Pay Board's calculations, but even the pro-Tory newspapers savaged Heath. It was a severe blow to the government, just as the election campaign was hotting up.

For Labour, the election was not about 'Who governs?' but about 'Getting Britain Back to Work'. We promised a quick, clean and honourable settlement of the miners' dispute. We pledged a new conciliation and arbitration set-up. And we claimed that Heath was using the miners as a smokescreen to hide the alarming and dangerous state of the economy. All of this was fair enough. Yet Labour's policies were far from satisfactory and our own proposals on the pay front in particular left a great deal to trust and goodwill.

Heath defeated

What happened was the familiar British election pattern. There was no great confidence in Her Majesty's Opposition, but there was a substantial no confidence vote in the government. It was an indecisive result, with the swing to Labour less than 1 per cent. Labour finished with 301 seats, only four more than the Tories. The Liberals, with fourteen seats, held the balance of power.

For the Tories, it could have been, and indeed should have been, far worse. Heath tried desperately to cobble up a deal with the Liberals to produce a coalition government. His undignified inability to do so was a further humiliation. The Queen asked Harold Wilson to form a government once more. Labour was back in charge.

Heath had been severely undermined by that damning Pay Board report, by sharp anti-government criticism by the CBI chief, Campbell Adamson, and by Enoch Powell's stab-in-the-back advice to vote Labour. (Powell refused to stand again as a Tory and denounced the election as 'an act of gross irresponsibility' and 'essentially fraudulent'. His influence with working-class voters was considerable and his proclamation was bound to damage the Tories.) But the biggest single factor in Heath's failure was his decision to tackle the unions, head-on. His reformist industrial relations policy never recovered from defeat by the miners in 1972. By 1974, after five states of emergency in three and a half years, his incomes policy was in tatters. Once more, the battle-hardened NUM struck the most deadly blow.

The unions did not govern, but they exercised an awesome negative power, having now napalmed their second successive government out of office. That they wanted their Labour allies back was not in doubt. But how long would their friendship, their support, last? How long would it be before their undeviating talent for self-destruction within the Labour movement was again unleashed? That uncertainty was to dominate the British political scene for the next five years. With friends like these. . . ?

5

Wilson Resuscitated

Instead of that all-embracing role in media matters which Harold Wilson suggested was likely for me in a Labour government, he appointed me as Parliamentary Secretary to the Civil Service Department, with the more limited task of co-ordinating government information services. It was certainly no sinecure. The way we got our message across promised to be vital in our precarious parliamentary position. Everything was coloured by the certainty that our minority government could not last, that another general election was bound to be upon us before the year was out and probably a good deal sooner than that.

Prime Minister Wilson asked me to set up and chair a weekly meeting of the 'Little Liaison Committee' – representatives from No. 10, from the office of Ted Short, the Lord President, from Transport House and from my own office. This revived a similar group which met in Wilson's earlier premiership under the chairmanship of Richard Crossman, the then Lord President. We sought to keep the government and the party in step, and to offer presentational advice to Short with which he could trundle off to Cabinet.

We kicked off with a senior level team. It included Joe Haines, Dr Bernard (now Lord) Donoughue and Marcia Williams, all from Wilson's staff, a top Transport House trio and Tom McNally, adviser to Jim Callaghan, the Party Chairman as well as Foreign Secretary.

The level of representation quickly fell away. Deputies appeared. Haines and Donoughue pleaded work pressure. Marcia was engulfed by the so-called slag-heaps affair. Her brother, Tony Field, former part-time office manager for Wilson, took part in a speculative land-deal investment. Wilson was dragged in through a letter, purporting to come from him but with a forged signature. Marcia's London mews home was

besieged by reporters and photographers. The 'Little Liaison Committee' understandably slipped from her agenda.

We needed a union input, so I got Wilson's approval to approach Len
Murray. Consequently, the rounded frying-pan face and outsize girth of
Norman Willis, the TUC's new Assistant General Secretary, became a
regular and relevant addition, especially useful when presentation of the
Social Contract between the government and the unions was such a
delicate issue.

One important element built into my post was involvement in
policy-making before final decisions were taken. I had the right to
attend most Cabinet committee meetings and to see all Cabinet
committee papers and most Cabinet papers. Some were top-secret
documents not available to all Cabinet members. The red despatch
boxes which went home with me each night were usually crammed with
enough Cabinet confidences to keep any of my old Fleet Street
newspaper chums in headlines for weeks ahead.

It was not long before I was disenchanted with the job. I was
supposed to nag and cajole senior ministers into co-operation over
themes for speeches and so on. In theory, I had prime ministerial say-so
to back me. In practice, obdurate Cabinet ministers needed a heavier
punch than I could muster if they were to comply. I spelled out on paper
and in a chat with Wilson my view that the job should be rethought for
the period after the forthcoming election. I also said that Labour should
start to turn 'open government' into a reality and should seek 'the
maximum flow of information consistent with secure and democratic
government'. I warned that there was 'a danger that the importance of
presentation will be somewhat disregarded by ministers should we
return to office with a "safe" majority'. I said that I would like a switch
after the election, assuming that we won, or else would prefer to revert
to the Back Benches.

The difficulties facing the incoming Labour government were
immense. There was a record balance of payments deficit and runaway
inflation, fuelled both by oil price rises and by Heath's wage threshold
agreements which doled out extra cash in line with the escalating Retail
Price Index.

It was bound to be a struggle but once the coal dispute was settled – to
the NUM's satisfaction – the new government moved rapidly to its first
Budget. Pensioners got their biggest rise since 1948. All other benefits
were increased, along with food and housing subsidies. Defence
spending was cut. There were higher taxes for the better-off and a raised

tax threshold to help the lower-paid. Price controls were announced. Nationalized industry prices were pegged back but some still soared. VAT and some indirect taxes went up sharply. A wealth tax was promised but remained a pipe-dream.

Labour and the unions

Labour forged its pre-election Social Contract with the unions, put it to the electors and could now seek to implement it. The Budget and other advances were designed to do just that. But the hard commitment was all on the government side of the deal. The union contribution was voluntary pay restraint, and even that was under fire from the Left.

The TUC did its best to keep the bargain. The General Council agreed that negotiators should only seek to match cost of living rises, and that was to include the otherwise inflationary threshold element. It was a considerable short-term achievement. Would it hold, though? Could it be built upon?

The unions were soon rewarded. Michael Foot, the Employment Secretary, introduced the Trade Union and Labour Relations Bill to repeal Heath's 1971 Act. The Bill abolished the National Industrial Relations Court, the Commission for Industrial Relations and the registry for unions and employers' associations. It restored to the unions their pre-1971 legal immunities in trade disputes and extended them in some respects. It legitimized the closed shop and scrapped the right not to belong to a union. It pledged a new-style arbitration and conciliation service, to be set up after consultation with the TUC and the CBI.

Privately, some union leaders thought that the clock was turned back too far, too fast. Foot was the darling of the Left but many of the union professionals remained highly sceptical. They reckoned that the government would have nothing left to bargain with if the going got rough, and they were right.

The Tories in disarray

The Tories were in a mess. Heath was fighting for his own political life as alternative leaders were canvassed. Du Cann, Prior, Sir Keith Joseph were possible contenders. Then there was Willie Whitelaw, whose bluff exterior hid a bluff interior. It was all very uninspiring. None of the political pundits gave Margaret Thatcher a thought.

The Conservative Party was down but not out. The leadership

mounted a sustained, belligerent and well-orchestrated crusade against us. We failed to match their brand of gang warfare. They were helped by a defeat or two for the government in Commons votes. A £10 million tax refund to the unions was scuppered and Labour's industry plans were thwarted. They were useful psychological boosts for the Tories, but really did little more than ensure an autumn polling date.

Nationalization was a key issue. Lord Hailsham led a Tory chorus against Benn and 'socialist dictatorship'. Shadow ministers conjured up a spine-chilling picture of a sinister Benn, heading some kind of industrial secret police force and taking over everything from British Leyland to the deckchairs on the Bournemouth seafront. Labour only had itself to blame. It failed to even consider presentation in launching its plans to establish the National Enterprise Board, planning agreements and the selective extension of public ownership, thus granting the Tories *carte blanche* for mischief-making.

The prime minister did pursue these matters within the Cabinet. As the election drew near, ministers became noticeably less sniffy about press releases and broadcasts. They were more presentation-conscious – or perhaps more concerned for their political skins. (The government couldn't limp along much longer without a fresh electoral mandate. Most of the betting was on October and all my work was in tune with that expectation.)

That July, Chancellor Denis Healey introduced a mini-Budget, aimed at cutting the still-rising Retail Price Index. His measures included a cut in VAT, higher domestic rate relief, increased rent allowances and more subsidies for food. Unemployment was a growing cause for concern and the regional employment premium was doubled to reduce labour costs.

At the TUC's conference in September, Prime Minister Wilson told the delegates: 'We cannot expect any significant increase in living standards overall in the next year or two. Indeed, it will be a tremendous challenge to our statesmanship even to maintain average living standards.' He didn't announce the election until two weeks later, but he made good use of the conference which endorsed the General Council's wage restraint recommendation.

Another election

The election was set for Thursday, 10 October 1974, and the campaign went off with little in the way of crises for Labour. (Wilson asked me to sit on the party's Campaign Committee and I spent much of the six-week-long contest at 10 Downing Street, 'ghosting' newspaper articles signed 'Harold Wilson' and helping with speech-writing.) Heath knew that the odds were against the Tories and that his own survival was at stake. He thrashed around for a viable vote-catching line and tried to pick up one peddled in parts of the media for a government of all the talents. He was guarded but he referred to a national government containing unaligned figures. Coming from the abrasive and self-opinionated Heath, it was hard to swallow.

There was a brief flurry when Labour's leading pro-Marketeers, Roy Jenkins and Shirley Williams, unbuttoned their dislike of Labour's pledge to hold a referendum of the British people to see whether we should remain within the Common Market on renegotiated terms. However, the issue soon evaporated in the general propaganda blizzard, and all the other effort Labour put into the campaign. The smart money was on a clear-cut Labour victory, but as it turned out, that was somewhat over-optimistic.

On 10 October Labour was returned to office but the overall majority was only four, allowing for the Speaker. There was a forty-three seat majority over the Conservatives – a gain of eighteen seats for Labour at Tory expense. It was a disappointingly slender success. It meant that the parliamentary pressure, the constant threat of defeat in the division lobbies, remained ever-present. Any minor rebellion against the Whip, Labour MPs caught up in a traffic snarl-up or rail delay, could wreck us. By-elections would be a major hazard. Still, Labour had made it back into office.

(My constituency gave me a 9,393 margin over the Tory candidate, the biggest majority since the war for Labour in either the former East or my current Central Islington seat. The only ugly note was the 1,335 votes cast for a National Front candidate.

Harold Wilson, safely reinstalled in Downing Street, made me a generous and most unusual, if not unique, offer for a junior minister. He recalled my request for a move and said that I could choose to be either Under-Secretary of State for Social Services, Army Minister or Parliamentary Secretary for Overseas Development. All three posts had equal status. I picked Overseas Development, where Judith Hart was the Minister. It was something which I never regretted.

It brought home to me powerfully, even painfully, the plight of millions throughout the developing world. It did so in a way that only first-hand experience can provide. Television has brought the suffering

71

vividly to all of us. But I walked among hordes of pitiful, starving children in the refugee camps, smelled the death and destitution and talked to those resolute and courageous people who devote their lives to the relief of this abject poverty and suffering.

I was quickly off on what turned into an eighteen-month crash course on Third World problems. My globe-trotting brought meetings with kings, presidents and premiers. There were British ambassadors and high commissioners whose 'old school tie' arrogance and bluff failed to mask their clueless inadequacies. And there were others, particularly the younger men and women, whose diplomatic skills and knowledge did our foreign service proud.

My most indelible memory is of a visit with Mother Teresa to her Calcutta homes for the dying and destitute. At one former ICI factory, the dying lay on mattresses on the concrete floors. All of them were cared for by cheerful and serene young Indian nuns in their white muslin dresses and by voluntary co-workers from around the world. As the remarkable Mother Teresa put it: 'This factory once made chemicals. Now it makes love.'

The Ministry of Overseas Development was often hectic, always enlightening. The backcloth of worldwide impoverishment made every triumph matter, however minimal. Judith Hart was passionately committed to the developing world and knew her stuff. She could be prickly and her relationship with the ODM's Permanent Secretary, Sir Richard King, the top civil servant there, was cool. They disliked each other and at one stage they were barely on speaking terms. I had to act as a sort of go-between.)

The Common Market campaign

In January 1975, Wilson announced that Labour would honour its pre-election pledge and would hold a referendum on Britain's Common Market membership, once renegotiation of our membership terms was complete. Labour's deep-seated internal difficulties would be overcome by allowing Cabinet members a free vote once a government recommendation was made. It was an ingenious compromise which angered the Tories who hoped for a breach in our ranks that would be impossible to heal.

Jim Callaghan, the Foreign Secretary, had Wilson's approval to set up a small informal group of pro-market ministers to meet daily under his chairmanship to co-ordinate presentation of the government's case on the referendum – the case for staying in the EEC. The existence of the group was never publicized.

Jim invited Shirley Williams, Bob Mellish, Bill Price (now in my old job at the Cabinet Office), David Ennals and Roy Hattersley (both Foreign Office ministers) and me. I was surprised to be included, but I discovered that Jim had no great faith in Bill Price, a lively but rather erratic former provincial journalist. As the campaign moved into its closing stages, Callaghan was able to report strong support for a 'Yes' vote. Wilson's personal popularity with the voters was higher than the government's and the pro-Market team sought to make good use of this. Some supposedly pro-Market ministers were reluctant to do much to promote the case for staying in. They knew that a 'Yes' vote made sense for Britain but preferred to keep out of Labour's domestic rumpus. Chancellor Healey kept a conspicuously low profile.

The unions were obstinately anti-Market but, as usual, their leaders' views were not reflected by the rank-and-file members who were as committed to the EEC as were the rest of the electorate – by 2–1 according to our private polls.

There were some weird alliances. Ian Mikardo, the veteran left-wing MP, said that Wilson led a 'motley multi-coloured army'. The leaders of the Labour, Conservative and Liberal parties all wanted a 'Yes' vote. Margaret Thatcher had ousted Heath as Tory leader, and the two now appeared together on the same platform to appeal to Tory MPs to back the pro-Market campaign. It was probably Thatcher's most pro-Market speech ever. The majority of opinion-formers in the media, the Civil Service and the universities, along with the City and industry, were pro-Marketeers.

As well as the unions, the 'anti' lobby also contained a majority of Labour's National Executive Committee who recommended a 'No' vote and were supported at a special party conference, held at the Sobell Centre in my London constituency. The 'antis' created a bizarre political kaleidoscope. There were the Far Right jingoists and xenophobics, the nationalists, the protectionists and the old-fashioned free-traders.

In June 1975, the electorate voted by 17,378,581 to stay within the EEC – a decisive 8,908,508 majority in a very satisfactory 64.5 per cent turn-out. *The Times* said that Harold Wilson's successful use of the referendum showed 'great political skill and insight'. He defused one of Labour's most heated feuds ever in a fashion that enhanced the party's electoral credibility.

The Social Contract

The Social Contract, though it wobbled violently during this period, still had the support of the TUC. This was due largely to Jack Jones who was a principal architect of the deal and thus wedded to its success.

The government declared its aim of getting inflation down to 10 per cent by the autumn of 1976 – ambitious enough when set against the 25 per cent annual rate of increase reached in the aftermath of Heath's inflationary statutory pay policy. There was agreement with the TUC on a £6 a week flat-rate minimum for rises and more than three million workers were covered by settlements within that limit by the end of 1975. But many pay deals lurched way beyond the inflation rate. They threatened to become frighteningly contagious and to place the entire policy in jeopardy.

The policy had its bitter critics, both inside the unions and in both the Labour and Conservative parties. The strains mounted. The economy drifted from crisis to crisis. The unions had all too few leaders who were ready to fight for what they knew was needed and all too many who kow-towed to their more militant activists. That was the case though few of them would have secured £6 a week more for their members by negotiation.

The unions could hardly complain that the Labour government had not kept its part of the bargain. Wilson trumpeted his achievement at the 1975 party conference in Blackpool. No previous Prime Minister, he said, had been able to present a record of a government which had carried through so much of its manifesto, by legislative and executive action, in so short a time. He spelled out thirty-five Bills and other measures which Labour had implemented during the short parliament of 1974. He produced another 'breathtaking' list for the year since the second 1974 election.

He pointed out that all this had only been possible through ministers and MPs working long into the night. That was true enough. The government's minuscule majority, further imperilled by death and defection, together with Tory guerrilla tactics meant constant nerve-tingling pressure. Ministers, the so-called 'payroll vote', were on virtual round-the-clock duty. There were early morning Cabinet committees, ministry meetings and other 'in-house' work, then to the Commons for more meetings and votes, often stretching well into the small hours.

Morale was pretty high, despite all the traumas, or perhaps because of them. Labour's social legislation offered much to be proud of, too much measured against the yardstick of our overseas creditors. Unfortunately, Labour was grievously undermined by the economic situation and the twin burdens of inflation and growing unemployment.

Wilson told the Labour conference that the unions and management must get more involved in the fight against inflation. 'Reflation cannot start', he said, 'before inflation stops.' He recognized that the extremists in our own ranks were crawling out of the woodwork to make trouble for the government. He spoke of 'infiltration' and 'infestation'.

(One major problem dropped on my ministerial doormat. In mid-1975, Wilson sacked Judith Hart and replaced her with Reg Prentice, until then the Education Secretary. Judith became too involved in Tony Wedgwood Benn's industrial policy extravagances for Wilson's liking. She did so ostensibly wearing her hat as a member of Labour's National Executive Committee, but she chose to ignore the storm signals and pushed her luck too far. I was sorry about her departure since I enjoyed working with her. Not that I had anxieties about Prentice, whom I had known for many years.

But Wilson sought to go further and to effectively scrap the ODM. It would be submerged within the Foreign Office. Judith had cleared her desk. Reg Prentice had yet to arrive and, in any event, was known to be primarily concerned with protecting his Cabinet status, no longer part of the ODM job, but awarded to him on a purely personal basis. His other understandable preoccupation was the fight in his East London constituency against an extremist take-over, a situation that led to his eventual defection to the Tories.

I fought a rearguard action to preserve the ODM, lobbying both Wilson and Callaghan. There was no apparent concession but when the plan was put into practice a separate identity was maintained. We became the Overseas Development Administration, though the Foreign Office was now our direct overlord. I like to think that my protestations had some effect.

Among my personal initiatives at the ODM was one involving the unions. I wanted an annual grant to the unions so that they could advise developing countries on union organization and work with them on social projects. If it was possible to nurture the growth of democratic trade unionism as a by-product in countries which rejected or merely paid lip-service to it, so much the better. I thought that our unions should be more aware of problems of the millions of hungry and destitute people around the world, and might begin to campaign on the issue as they did for pensioners at home. I had extensive talks with Len

Murray and his TUC colleagues and set up the necessary mechanism. The final approval came through after I had moved on, but an annual grant to the TUC for use in developing countries continues to be made.)

Wilson's resignation

On 16 March 1976 Wilson resigned. He was not a man to whom one could easily warm, but his achievements were considerable and his overall contribution to British politics generally, and to the Labour Party in particular, has never been adequately acknowledged.

In his post-resignation minute to the Cabinet, Harold Wilson explained that in March 1974 he vowed that he would remain in office for no more than two years. He had not wavered from that decision. There have been many theories, some remarkably far-fetched, as to why he decided to retire. I am among those who knew him well and subscribe to the simple belief that there was no mystery, that he had quite simply had enough. No one has come up with an even remotely credible alternative proposition.

6

Jim Can't Fix It

Jim Callaghan's premiership promised improved relations with the unions. Most of the union barons got on well enough with Harold Wilson but they never fully trusted him or felt that he was out of the same stable.

Jim, one-time official of the Inland Revenue Staff Federation (the taxmen's union), and former parliamentary adviser to the Police Federation, had an apparent rapport with the unions. He championed their cause during the 'In Place of Strife' débâcle. He understood them and would carry them with him.

That was the superficial assessment. The reality was that, whatever the outward appearance, there were few genuinely close relationships between union leaders and senior members of the government, and that included Prime Minister Callaghan. Moreover, his avuncular image masked an underlying severity and cussedness which contrasted sharply with the familiar Wilson tendency to haggle and seek compromise. Now that Jim had a government to run it would all be very different from his wily pro-union manœuvring in the late sixties. There were storms ahead.

Callaghan reshuffled the government as soon as he took over. He asked me to switch from Overseas Development to my natural habitat – the Department of Employment. He said that he wanted my experience there in what were bound to be difficult times. He explained that Michael Foot, now Labour's Deputy Leader and the new Lord President and Leader of the Commons, insisted on a leg-up for those he left behind at Employment. That elevated Albert Booth to be Secretary of State, with Harold Walker as Minister of State. Jim gave the distinct impression that he would have preferred a different set-up but was not going to annoy Foot, once a political enemy but now a vital ally.

My new responsibilities included industrial health and safety, employment of the disabled, equal opportunities, low pay and EEC and overseas matters, this latter a logical follow-on from my ODA duties. I represented the British government at every meeting of EEC Labour and Social Affairs ministers in Brussels and Luxembourg. These were the days when the French were the 'no-men' of Europe and painfully so. Their obstruction, based on blatant and rigid self-interest, was a constant irritation.

The Race Relations Act

I was plunged straight into the 1976 Race Relations Bill which had already had its second reading debate in the Commons and was due to start its committee stage. This sensitive legislation was primarily a Home Office baby but there were important employment aspects. One of my closest parliamentary friends, the late Brynmor John, the Home Office Minister of State, led on the Bill. I was the second minister involved and handled the many clauses about discrimination at the workplace and related matters.

This was the first of many chances during the next three years for me to do all that I could towards preventing racial discrimination in employment – in personnel procedures like recruitment and promotion, by leaning on public and private sector employers to do better and by chivvying the unions, where there was far more lip-service paid to the need for shop-floor action than there was effort expended.

At that time a black unskilled worker had a one-in-two chance of running into discrimination when applying for a job. The chance of discrimination against a black white-collar worker was one-in-three. The cards were heavily stacked against ethnic minority school-leavers. The 1976 legislation was aimed at combating this and especially at indirect discrimination, often unintentional but equally harmful. For example, employers could no longer impose on job applicants requirements which, though not explicit, effectively barred blacks. No law could guarantee reform but we produced a framework to help and one which we hoped would change attitudes.

Inside the Commons committee, the Tory backbenchers were mostly those who wanted an improved race relations climate. Willie Whitelaw, the Shadow Home Secretary, was helpful, and the committee proceedings were largely uneventful. Back on the floor of the House, however, the Tory backwoodsmen crawled out of the parliamentary undergrowth. Whitelaw, who favoured the principles which the Bill enshrined, strode in and out of the chamber with a face like thunder as his tortuous party colleagues, together with the ever-obnoxious Enoch Powell, filibustered on, beyond control, in their vain attempt to wreck the Bill. Not that Whitelaw disassociated himself as firmly as he might have done from the unwholesome crew behind him on the Tory benches. He appeared to be uncomfortably aware of the need to avoid a head-on collision with his party's racist wing.

The futile word-spinning and sniping went on for twenty-one hours. Labour Backbenchers choked back their speeches, restrained by the knowledge that time is the enemy of parliamentary progress. Eventually, the Tories wilted. The Bill got its necessary third reading. It was not much longer reaching the statute book. Only the National Front and similar extremists could have drawn comfort from the unsavoury Tory rebellion.

The new legislation was there to be built upon. The government was committed to tackling discrimination among firms with which it placed contracts. I sought to insist that all government contractors should supply the Employment Department with details of their employment policies and practices. That would allow monitoring to ensure that they employed blacks and other ethnic minorities. Contract compliance on these lines was part of the original scheme in the Government White Paper which preceded the Bill.

It took until 1979 to get anywhere with this. The Treasury and the spending departments, like the Department of the Environment, were all opposed to anything that might add to costs, not just industry's but also to those of the government as a major employer. The CBI was hostile to contract compliance. So was the Cabinet committee which considered my explicit proposals. Expected allies failed to materialize, despite my advance lobbying of selected ministerial friends. I looked like losing the lot but Merlyn Rees, the Home Secretary, chairing the meeting, and Shirley Williams, showed some sympathy.

I was able to announce that government contractors would have to give the Employment Department details of their policies to eliminate unlawful discrimination where we requested it. I said that this should cause no fuss or anxiety 'unless employers are either entrenched in complacency or have something to hide'. Even this footling compromise was overtaken by the subsequent change of government and vanished.

The 1976 Race Relations Act signalled a radical advance on the race relations front. The spirit of that legislation, never adequately fostered, has all but gone. The present government's support for the Commission for Racial Equality, established by the Act, has been grudging. Where experience indicates that the law needs strengthening – for instance, on indirect discrimination in employment and for ethnic monitoring – the government has backed away. Discrimination at work is not much different now to the unhappy mid-seventies situation – a manifest reproof for years of hypocritical pretence to progress.

The disabled

There was particular job satisfaction in dealing with the employment problems of the disabled and working closely with the Manpower Services Commission to introduce or improve on schemes ranging from providing special aids for the severely handicapped at work to helping with fares to get disabled people to the workplace. I argued fiercely to achieve preferential treatment for disabled people within the government's job release scheme. I wanted the age of eligibility cut to sixty (it was sixty-two for the able-bodied) to give disabled people the chance of early retirement and to provide new job openings for unemployed disabled people. DHSS civil servants – and apparently ministers – were opposed to this. So too were our own civil servants, not in principle, but because they believed that victory on this might jeopardize their proposals to go to the Treasury for more spending elsewhere. I persuaded Albert Booth to fix a meeting with DHSS ministers. No civil servants. We met in the Commons with Stan Orme, the Social Security Minister, and Alf Morris, Minister for the Disabled. Free from inhibiting Civil Service advice, my proposal was readily agreed.

There was another battle over the sheltered workshops which employ disabled people. I thought that they should have far greater priority when public-sector contracts were awarded. A Cabinet committee considered this and, having softened up enough ministerial chums, I achieved my objective. It was necessary to keep up a constant offensive on behalf of the disabled, both through public exhortation and private pressure, and it was gratifying that my Employment Department days saw a worthwhile increase in manpower and resources devoted to the disabled.

Health and safety

Health and safety provided another carefully contrived behind-the-scenes success, thanks to a union push. The government was supposed to introduce regulations in the Commons that would enable the appointment of workplace trade union safety representatives and safety committees. Human tragedies apart, there were, and still are, enormous economic losses through accidents at work. The cost in lost production, industrial injury benefit and so on, runs into hundreds of millions of pounds annually. The Health and Safety Commission, the TUC and the CBI supported the introduction of the regulations. The government, however, pussyfooted around, and civil servants reported adamant opposition, as usual, from the Treasury and from the spending departments, notably Environment and the DHSS. Albert Booth was due to take our proposals to Cabinet and the odds were stacking up against him. A counter-attack was needed. I let the *Guardian* know that the regulations were likely to be scuppered in Cabinet. A brief back-page piece appeared on the Monday before the Thursday Cabinet which would make the decision. TUC officials were soon on the phone to my office, alarmed at the newspaper report. I talked to Jack Jones and urged a TUC initiative. He got cracking at a meeting of the TUC's 'inner cabinet', the Finance and General Purposes Committee, that same afternoon. The result was an eve-of-Cabinet TUC protest delegation, led by Len Murray, to Downing Street to see the Prime Minister.

Those regulations came up next morning at Cabinet. Jim Callaghan said immediately that they should go ahead. A few Civil Service briefs to ministers were hurriedly shuffled away, and no one demurred. Albert discreetly said nothing. It was acceptance on the nod. It was evidence that the TUC still had influence, of the power of the press – and of a spot of ministerial stage management, too.

National Advisory Council for the Employment of Women

On the question of appointments to the National Advisory Council for the Employment of Women (a worthy-sounding body, comprised of worthy people from the unions, employers' organizations and academia, offering staid, studied and undoubtedly worthy advice), I drew with the civil servants. I inherited the chairmanship of this body, and a dull meeting or two convinced me that it needed enlivening. So I decided to add a non-establishment name or two. I picked Patricia

Hewitt, then General Secretary of the National Council for Civil Liberties, and the left-wing journalist Anna Coote. The formidable lady civil servant responsible for the Advisory Council's role came to see me, grimly determined to stop this ministerial nonsense. I dug in my heels, but eventually we came to a compromise. It was not worth creating ill will, so I settled for Hewitt, later Neil Kinnock's Parliamentary Press Secretary, who was bright and articulate. (So articulate, in fact, that she simply didn't know when to shut up. It must have been quite a contest when she was in tandem with the loquacious Kinnock.)

Wages councils

Wages councils took up a lot of time. The councils set minimum standards of pay and conditions for some three million low-paid workers in industries where union organization is either poor or non-existent. The unions have been traditionally uninterested in helping these non-members or the relatively few unionized employees, scattered around in small 'sweatshop' firms and thus disproportionately expensive to organize and to service.

The government's £6 pay limit was designed to help the low paid, and did so to good effect for those in wages council industries, who were mostly on subsistence living standards. Most awards for these workers in that period were at or near to the full £6 a week and meant rises of 20–25 per cent, far more than their customary level of settlement.

There was widespread underpayment by employers in wages council industries – 'the pickpockets of industry, the back-street brigade, pinching from the pay packets of those who can least afford to be done down in this way', I said in a Commons debate. It was easy enough to condemn. But the size of the wages inspectorate responsible for policing wages council awards had yet to be restored after severe cuts in its establishment made by the Heath government. Our government too, was trying to prune back civil service manpower. So I could promise nothing concrete that would improve on the pathetic inspection rate, which was a pity, since we needed to get round the manpower shortage and make both employers and employees more aware of their respective obligations and rights. Ignorance of the often absurdly complicated wages council orders was more to blame for default by employers than was deliberate evasion.

We launched a 'blitz' campaign, concentrating our inspectorate's work through surprise raids on employers in selected towns. There

George Brown, Secretary of State for Economic Affairs, holds up a copy of the Joint Statement of Intent on Productivity, Prices and Incomes, concluded between the Labour Government, employers and union leaders, 1964.

George Brown, Labour's Secretary of State for Economic Affairs, hammers home the case for a prices and incomes policy to the ETU's Isle of Man delegate conference in 1965. ETU President Les Cannon is on his left and General Secretary Frank Chapple is on his right.

The author and his wife, Pat, at a Labour Party dinner in the mid-60s with Frank and Nance Cousins.

TUC General Secretary George Woodcock. What are we here for – and where are we going?

Two of the author's trade union friends, Frank Chapple (left) and Joe Gormley.

General election 1979 – a Labour Party headquarters press conference with employment and industrial relations as its theme. Left to right: Harold Walker, Employment Minister of State; Prime Minister James Callaghan; Labour's General Secretary Ron Hayward; and the author.

"ON YOUR BIKE!"

Sun cartoonist Franklin illustrates the split in the SDP over Norman Tebbit's 1982 Industrial Relations Bill and shows the author leading the 'anti-Tebbit' group of SDP MPs. (No, not the little fellow perched on the handlebars.)

Electioneering – and pleasantly so.

Industry Secretary Norman Tebbit visits the EETPU's Cudham, Kent, technical training centre. Left to right: EETPU General Secretary Eric Hammond, Norman Tebbit, and the author.

Meeting the press and in defiant mood, prior to the EETPU's 1988 expulsion from the TUC. At the table (left to right): the author, EETPU General Secretary Eric Hammond, and President Paul Gallagher.

Expelled from the TUC. The EETPU delegation on its way from the 1988 TUC conference.

With SDP Leader Dr David Owen.

were some Civil Service misgivings about this. It was hardly the stuff of bureaucracy. But the inspectors soon got into the swing of it. It meant a fall in the overall inspection rate across the country, but publicity for the 'blitz' was certain. That would put the wages councils and the inspectorate on the map. The deterrent value would be considerable. Arrears would be recovered from employers in the towns that were hit, but prosecutions, a hugely expensive use of inspectors' time, would be restricted to blatant and persistent offenders.

We certainly made the headlines on this question, and there were front-page stories in the national newspapers, and a variety of comment – not all of it friendly. The 'blitz' was reasonably successful. The first swoop in 1976 brought £76,000 in arrears to workers in twenty-three towns where more than a quarter of employers were found to be underpaying. We carried on, and in 1977 the inspectorate recovered a record £1,600,000 for underpaid employees. There were seven prosecutions, compared with none in 1976. In 1978, there were more prosecutions. Better still, I was able to report a 10 per cent increase in the 150-strong force of inspectors. Nor did they any longer have to handle the employment disablement quota scheme, a change that equalled another 10 per cent rise in their establishment. It meant that the Heath cuts were restored. We took steps, too, to make wages council awards more intelligible and to help home-workers.

There is, unfortunately, little to show for all this today. The inspectorate numbers have been slashed and the inspection rate of employers' premises has plummeted. Underpayment is reckoned to be worse than ever. Wages councils are threatened with abolition. So far, they have mostly survived, but their impact is less than it ever was and their future remains imperilled.

Footballers and work permits

The biggest onslaught of adverse publicity which I ran into was over the most inconsequential of issues – work permits for overseas footballers. The rise in unemployment had resulted in a good deal of understandable pressure, not least from the unions, to reduce the inflow of foreign workers. The Professional Footballers' Association (PFA) was in the vanguard of those seeking more restriction and we could not ignore the case strongly advanced by the PFA to protect the employment opportunities of our home-grown soccer talent. There were no half-measures for the PFA, which demanded a total ban on non-EEC players. That went too far, so I said that no further work permits would go to non-EEC overseas footballers until DE officials completed consultations with the various British football authorities.

I exempted applications already in the pipeline after anguished appeals by Tottenham Hotspur and Southampton. Spurs sought to bring in Ricky Villa and Ossie Ardiles, from Argentina. Southampton's quarry was Ivan Golac, the Yugoslav fullback. Tottenham's MP, Norman Atkinson, pleaded Spurs' case. So did Lord Ted Willis, Labour peer, author, playwright, dedicated Spurs fan and a firm personal friend ever since. All three players were quality internationals and it seemed harsh to bring down the axe when everything but the work permits had been settled in good faith. This trio went on to contribute considerably to our footballing scene and to public entertainment.

Our talks with the football authorities led to rejection of the call for an outright ban. That would have put football into a different category to every other industry. I decided on strict application of the existing work permit scheme's criteria to professional football. Permits would only go to overseas players of established international reputation who could make 'a distinctive contribution' to our game.

All was well until the Scottish club, Hibernian, asked for permits for two Norwegians, Svein Mathison and Isak Refvik. Our officials doubted whether either player met the criteria. While we pondered Hibs tried a *fait accompli*. They invited both men in as 'visitors' and signed them on amateur forms. They enlisted the Scottish press as allies, and there were headlines about this 'Scrooge' English minister who threatened to discriminate against a Scottish club.

It turned into quite a campaign, one which Scots politicians did their best to fuel. I was angrily accosted in the Commons dining room by Bruce Millan, the Secretary of State for Scotland. Millan (now a Euro-commissioner) demanded to know what I thought I was doing. 'You'll lose us the election in Scotland,' he declared. He was serious, and was responding to an increasingly frenzied Scottish media and to Scots MPs, Labour as well as those from opposition parties. I was all the more determined to resist. There was, though, a genuine case for Mathison which I accepted. Refvik got a turndown and I publicly rebuked Hibs for tricky footwork. I pointed out that a Commons select committee and the Tory Opposition were calling for stricter application of work permit rules. But the last laugh was mine. Neither Norwegian made the first team grade with Hibs. It was not long before they were both back in Norway.

Credit to Albert Booth. There was no interference from him. Whenever I sought his backing over difficult departmental decisions, I got it. With his yeoman's face and cumbersome homespun style, he lacked public charisma and was no potent force within the Cabinet. But he was a workhorse, thorough and strong on detail. His leftwing tendencies were loyally submerged on pay policy issues though, like me, he always showed extra concern for the low paid. He was no compelling figure but he had an honesty of purpose that is not the most noteworthy characteristic among senior politicians.

Pay policy

Throughout my time at the Employment Department I was preoccupied with the fate of pay policy. Combative enjoyment and incurable anxiety ensured that I was up to my neck in the overall situation rather than confined to my specific low-pay portfolio. I wrote and spoke about the policy wherever and whenever I could acquire a platform. There were many ministers who maintained a discreet and contemptible silence when they should have weighed in forcefully on behalf of a government under siege. Some of those who kept their heads down were inside the Cabinet. Junior ministers were not encouraged to be controversial on such a sensitive matter. I would never get Downing Street clearance for the kind of aggressive newspaper article that Cabinet ministers neglected to present. So I penned a thousand-word statement to my local Labour Party which, I told them, would be too long to include in my regular oral report to the General Management Committee. I sent a copy to the *Guardian* which ran it at length under the heading 'Enter Stage Four?'

My statement lambasted free collective bargaining and those union leaders who had grown tired of the struggle for restraint. I rejected the growing union demand for an 'orderly return' to a wages-free-for-all as 'an orderly return to chaos'. Freedom for worker to exploit worker. I defended the Social Contract and complained that 'not enough of those who think this way have stood up to be counted – in the government, the party or the unions'.

Next day the phone line buzzed from 10 Downing Street to my own Private Office. The format – that statement to my local party – covered my back but it was made plain that I should have asked permission before allowing the *Guardian* to launch my assault on our fainthearts and our detractors. Another attack seemed like the best form of defence.

I put in a written request to No. 10, via my private secretary, to let the left-wing weekly *Tribune* reprint my *Guardian* article. Callaghan's private secretary replied tersely: 'The Prime Minister would not want your Minister to publish this article or to write a shortened version of the article for *Tribune.*' The stable door slammed shut but the horse had already bolted. My initial instincts were right. I would never have got the all-clear for publication in the first place. It was better to have published and been damned.

Superficially at least, the government began to have reasons for cautious optimism. The TUC continued to back the pay guidelines and inflation dropped to 7 per cent – 20 per cent less than the 1975 peak. Tension though, mounted. An impending rift emerged in July 1977, when Jack Jones failed with an impassioned plea to the TGWU's biennial conference to sustain the Social Contract and pay restraint. Such a momentous defeat for a TGWU General Secretary by his members was unprecedented. It plunged the biggest union into conflict with the government.

I had an informal chat with Alan Fisher, leader of the National Union of Public Employees. He was a friendly, cheerful and likeable man, whom I had known for many years. He was subsequently branded as the union leader who did most to bring down the Callaghan government – a charge that was hard for him to refute. Yet Fisher was no natural militant. He was a longstanding supporter of the kind of pay policy that would aid his low-paid members. His energy and organizing ability were instrumental in NUPE's phenomenal growth – from 280,000 members to 700,000 during his period of leadership. But Alan was also a platform hothead who was increasingly influenced by the Left within his ranks, not least among his full-time officials.

At this time he was still trying to be helpful to the government. I minuted Albert Booth to seek urgent attention for Fisher's private views on two simmering disputes – for local authority manual workers and for hospital ancillary workers. NUPE had voted against accepting the employers' offers but I told Booth that Fisher was anxious to avoid industrial action. I asked for a statement from the Prime Minister or Chancellor of the Exchequer which acknowledged that 'there is a low-pay problem which needs to be looked at when times are better'. It wasn't seeking much but it would help Fisher with his own Executive Council and at the forthcoming area conferences which he was due to face. There was no firm commitment involved. I said that the hospital workers' case was more dangerous and that Fisher assured me of 'very real militancy here with the Socialist Workers' Party and other fringe groups very active and awaiting their chance'. I stressed that Fisher – 'who incidentally, shares my views on incomes policy' – had done no more than 'warn us of the dangers and plead for any possible flexibility at the margins'.

The 5 per cent policy

Despite warning signs of the massive industrial eruption to come, Callaghan, Healey, Foot and the rest of the Cabinet were strangely complacent prior to the 1978–79 pay round. They were cheered somewhat, even lulled, by those traces of economic recovery. It was, Callaghan boldly predicted, to be the country's Year of Recovery. He had already speculated about a 5 per cent inflation rate for 1979, and that was to be hardened into a 5 per cent pay limit – a line that could never be held after the preceding years of severe restraint. Not for sure, without a commitment, enthusiasm and toughness that simply didn't exist – neither in the unions nor in the ranks of the government. Most union leaders were tired of selling restraint to their members and cynical about the results. There was fertile ground for their ever-present militants to till, and the jobs of some moderates were endangered when they sought re-election. Nor were ministers setting an example by getting out on the stump to ram home the government case. That 5 per cent policy proved to be the keystone that wrecked the arch.

A false sense of security prevailed. Labour was neck-and-neck with the Tories in the public opinion polls. Confrontation with the unions had yet to materialize. Unemployment stayed stubbornly high, but there was a favourable look to pay and price inflation, to the strength of sterling, to the balance of payments, to general interest and mortgage rates and to industrial investment forecasts. The 1978 Budget brought rises in pensions, child benefit, a freeze on school meal prices, the restoration of free school milk for under-elevens and extra help for small firms, for health services and for schools.

Labour's prospects in an autumn election looked fair, but timing was all. Pay remained the powder-keg. Union leaders warned Callaghan that they had had enough, that the situation was explosive. The government's economic needs and the industrial facts of life were fast becoming incompatible, and Callaghan did not have the kind of parliamentary majority to see him through. The formal Lib–Lab pact had ended after eighteen months, though it was a friendly break.

The Liberals too, expected an autumn election and wanted time to re-establish their own identity. They continued to back Labour on most key issues, but it was hazardous hand-to-mouth stuff. Left-wing Labour MPs seethed with discontent. Only fear of defeat in an early election, which their defiance could precipitate, kept them in check.

Callaghan's 5 per cent ploy was supported by Chancellor Denis Healey, whose advice from some Treasury civil servants was for an even lower norm, stringently applied. Callaghan too, wanted to turn the pay policy screw. He believed that the Employment Department, traditionally close to the unions, showed signs of slackness, even feebleness, in its incomes policy approach. He needed a scapegoat. He picked on Sir Kenneth Barnes, our Permanent Secretary, an unfailingly genial, urbane and dedicated civil servant, who did his job quietly but firmly. Too quietly, perhaps. Only an anguished intervention by Albert Booth, who shot off to see the Prime Minister at No. 10, rescued Sir Kenneth in what has long been one of Whitehall's best-kept secrets. It was another creditable action by Booth.

In July 1978, the government produced its new White Paper, 'Winning the Battle Against Inflation'. From 1 August the total rise for any group, compared with the previous year, was pegged to that 5 per cent maximum. There were exceptions for self-financing productivity deals and for low pay (where earnings were no more than £44.50 for a normal full-time week). There were a small number of special cases where more was allowed – firemen, police and the Armed Forces. The White Paper called for a long-term approach in which collective bargaining was based each year on a broad agreement between government, unions and employers about the level of earnings compatible with keeping inflation under control.

There was no negotiation with the unions, Wilson-style, and no window-dressing. It was a chastening experience for the TUC. The Congress House influence on government policy had been immense. The Social Contract gave the unions unaccountable power at the core of our democratic system.

Now they suffered a shattering disillusion. The TUC, aggrieved by the perceived snub, gave a clear thumbs-down to the 5 per cent norm. Perhaps they would have swallowed it – unlikely but possible. They never expected though, that it would have time to take effect. They anticipated a general election before the new policy could bite into the 1978–79 pay round. It was one more error, pardonable, but ultimately fatal.

On the eve of the September 1978 Trades Union Congress at Brighton, Jim Callaghan invited the so-called 'Neddy Six', the TUC members of the National Economic Development Council, to dinner at his Sussex farmhouse. He sounded out each of them for their view of the forthcoming pay round and on the timing of the election. Only the engineers' left-wing president, Hugh Scanlon, was for delay. The rest forecast a winter of bouts and bloodshed. They urged the prime minister to go to the country swiftly.

(I was one of the few Ministers attending the Brighton conference. I sat next to Denis Healey in the visitors' gallery to hear the Callaghan speech to the delegates. Denis asked me for my view of the election timing. I was adamant. 'We should go now. There's trouble piling up.' Denis merely nodded a non-committal response. I was not to know that the decision to delay had already been taken, that Denis agreed with it, and that the arch-ditherer, Michael Foot, was even more anxious to hang on.)

Jim Callaghan went on to tease the conference. Warbling 'Waiting at the church' might have been a useful wheeze to get the delegates in good humour but it left the bulk of the TUC General Council in dismay. On television later that week, he confirmed that there would be no autumn election. It was a disastrous move, as the writing on the wall was crude and unmistakeable, but Callaghan and his senior Cabinet colleagues would not read it.

By late September, the Ford car strike was under way after union rejection of a wage offer within the government's guidelines. But Chancellor Healey, in Washington for meetings of the International Monetary Fund and the World Bank, presented a buoyant view of the UK economy and was bullish about its prospects. He predicted single-figure inflation throughout 1979, with the earnings out-turn at 7 per cent, allowing 2 per cent for self-financing productivity agreements and for slippage on top of the 5 per cent ceiling.

His optimism had scant effect on the union-dominated Labour Party conference a few days later. It overwhelmingly rejected pay restraint, just as the TUC had done before it. There were some fighting speeches from pay policy supporters such as Sid Weighell, of the NUR, and the postmen's Tom Jackson. Their minority case won the argument but was unable to sway the predetermined block votes. Sid Weighell angered the Left with a fierce attack on the 'pig trough' philosophy of those advocating a wages free-for-all.

Moss Evans had replaced Jack Jones at the TGWU. He was a

pleasant, affable man, but a political weakling. The Left had won a unique victory over the redoubtable Jones, and Evans, no left-winger from conviction, was easy meat for them. It showed in his conference performance. Not that there was any simple Left–Right split. Customary moderates like Joe Gormley, of the miners, and the engineers' Gavin Laird, opposed the government's norm.

Jim Callaghan told the conference that the rebuff was 'a lesson in democracy'. He knew that it was really a lesson in futility. He went on to remind the delegates of the government's successes, including the lasting single-figure inflation which the Tories insisted was impossible under Labour. He appealed for responsible bargaining, then declared, to applause, that it was the government's inescapable task to keep down inflation in the interests of the whole country. His nuts-and-bolts lecture contained a blunt warning that unacceptable wage inflation due to weakened pay policy would mean other government measures, monetary and fiscal, that would hit jobs.

He offered new talks with the unions 'to see where we move from here . . . to find a better way to resolve the issue of pay levels'. Denis Healey and the TUC's negotiators cobbled together a form of words to paper over the cracks arising from those TUC and Labour conference decisions. It was a weak and woolly document. No pay norm or ceiling was mentioned. Damage limitation was the name of the game, rather than any successful new beginning. Yet the TUC General Council, with several moderates needlessly and foolishly missing, split down the middle. The ultra-modest proposals fell. The government could only soldier on despairingly with the White Paper version of incomes policy, 5 per cent norm and all. This time the fault lay squarely with the TUC. It was asked to do very little and, typically, proved unsuccessful, even at failure.

A week later the nine-week strike at Ford ended with a 17 per cent pay deal. The government sought to use its sanctions against Ford, but, in a night of shame, it lost the crucial Commons vote. Left-wing Labour MPs deserted. Once again, there was gross mishandling, if not cowardice, by the Labour leadership. Earlier that day, I canvassed for a vote of confidence. Our left-wing rebels would have come into line rather than bring the government down, an act for which they would have been answerable not only to ordinary party members but also to the electorate. Our incomes policy would have remained intact. (My position was regarded as heretical by most colleagues. Of those ministers I spoke to, only the Transport Minister, Bill Rodgers, agreed with me. A few right-wing ministers did meet privately to discuss a confidence vote, but later chickened out.)

Next day, the government won a ritual vote of confidence, a formal necessity after its defeat over sanctions. Pay policy though, was effectively over. Sanctions could no longer be sustained, and it was the beginning of the end for the Labour government.

The Winter of Discontent

The Winter of Discontent loomed. One after another, groups of disgruntled workers used their muscle to secure hefty rises which mocked Callaghan's norm. They poured through the gaping hole in the government's defences which was created by the absence of sanctions. BBC technicians and other employees got 15 per cent rises after threatening a Christmas television black-out. An oil-tanker drivers' dispute ended with rises of 13 to 15 per cent. These were mere titbits, foretastes of the horror to come. They were swiftly exceeded by violent picketing in a road haulage strike.

In mid-January 1979, the government modified its 5 per cent limit to an unofficial and unacknowledged 8 per cent, and accepted that there should be pay comparability. Who cared? The remnants of the Social Contract vanished under a wave of savage industrial disruption and inflationary settlements which left for dead any government guideline, official or otherwise.

The lorry drivers won 17–20 per cent more, as the Winter of Discontent moved from dispute to dispute towards its unpalatable climax. Local authority manual workers began a prolonged campaign of industrial action, which antagonized and alienated the public, and, at the same time, paved the way for Margaret Thatcher.

There was a day-long stoppage by public-sector workers, ranging from grave-diggers to hospital porters. This was followed by a series of regional strikes. Hospital wards were forced to close, corpses awaited burial and rats feasted on the stinking, rotten refuse piled up on the streets. The 'dirty jobs' dispute found Alan Fisher's NUPE in the vanguard of militancy, with the TGWU and the General and Municipal Workers' Union not far behind.

Acres of media space devoted to our menacing industrial troubles fed the egos and fuelled the obstinacy of all those directly involved. NUPE officials were quick to tip off eager journalists about the most lurid stories to illustrate the union's impact, however damaging to the public's perception of trade unionism, now seen as cruel and brutish. The Tory tabloid press, in particular, had plenty to show for their efforts. It was highly emotive stuff, facilitated by those who customarily condemned this kind of journalism. Double standards were at a premium.

Water and sewage workers rejected a 14 per cent offer. Miners and power workers joined the scramble with 40 per cent pay demands. The teachers plumped for 35 per cent. It was senseless profligacy. The sky was fast becoming the limit. As the strikes went on, Jim Callaghan talked of 'vandals'. Frank Chapple spoke of 'terrorism, not trade unionism' on the picket lines, and was needlessly rebuked by the TUC's Len Murray for talking 'dangerous nonsense'.

'A Better Way'

I initiated another 'private enterprise' bid for change. After Labour's disastrous Blackpool conference, I sounded out Sid Weighell, Tom Jackson and one or two other pro-incomes policy union moderates to see what could be done to switch that 1978 pay policy verdict by the TUC and Labour conferences by securing a reversal at the 1979 gatherings. To do so meant campaigning at the 1979 round of individual union policy-making conferences during the spring and summer, for it was at these conferences that the key decisions would be taken on how to cast the block votes at the subsequent TUC and Labour get-togethers.

It was essential that any new initiative was seen as coming from the unions, not the government. Nor could I have expected any formal approval for this risky venture which could easily backfire. But I reckoned that my personal bonds with union leaders and my journalistic know-how would enable me to get something going, and possibly bring it to fruition. It was worth a try.

So I got together a small group who met during that turbulent winter, usually for a working dinner at one of London's railway hotels. Along with Weighell and Jackson, were Tony Christopher (from the Inland Revenue Staff Federation), Terry Duffy (the engineers' president and successor to Hugh Scanlon), Geoffrey Drain (from NALGO) and the steelworkers' Bill Sirs.

The end product was a thirteen-page pamphlet, 'A Better Way', in which the signatories called for a new voluntary pay policy and a far tougher prices policy. It suggested:

(1) tripartite annual talks between unions, employers and the government to set an 'indicative norm' for pay which allowed for wage drift and for justifiable above-the-norm rises;
(2) a revived central advisory role on pay for the TUC;
(3) a new independent agency, on the lines of the former Prices and Incomes Board, to apply the policy to pay, prices, profits and dividends;
(4) much tougher government powers to freeze or cut prices;
(5) an investigation of European-style share-ownership schemes.

'A Better Way' rejected the 'sterile dogma' of the monetarists and other economic extremists. It declared that if the Labour movement could not set its own priorities to the extent which we outlined, then 'trade union brotherhood and democratic socialism together have failed to live up to their proud ideals'. An initial 2,000 free copies of the document were sent to all TUC-affiliated unions, to trades councils, to constituency Labour parties and to Labour MPs, calling on both the unions and the party to revert to 'a sensible, coherent and responsible approach'.

I persuaded leaders of some of the biggest unions to come on board. TUC Chairman Tom Jackson (of the postmen's union) was an enthusiast – and a big help with distribution and postage. Sid Weighell, too, gave firm support, as did Leif Mills (of the bank employees) and the clerical workers' Roy Grantham.

Lord Alf Allen, from USDAW, the shopworkers' union, was important, as he chaired the TUC Economic Committee. He was scrupulous and not inclined towards 'unofficial' action of any kind. Thus I spent hours on the phone to him, discussing the draft, before he signed up. Nor was Frank Chapple really an incomes policy man, and he complained bitterly at the effect of the government's squeeze on the differentials of his skilled electrician members. The document's preamble made plain that those signing did so in their personal capacities, not necessarily supporting all it contained but believing that the overall case should be advanced. That – and our personal friendship – was good enough for Frank.

The Civil and Public Service Association's Ken Thomas took a fair amount of flak from the union's left wing for joining us. But a more surprising signatory was Jack Boddy, of the agricultural workers' union. He was a left-winger, but accepted the need for fresh moves to quell the growing chaos and the consequential damage to the living standards of those, such as his members, on low pay and without industrial strength.

Other moderate union leaders were, for various reasons, including cowardice, unwilling to sign. Still, we got a dozen useful signatories from sizeable TUC-affiliated organizations, and the pamphlet, quickly dubbed 'the moderates' manifesto', had an excellent press. The *Birmingham Post* called it 'a breath of fresh air'. The *Guardian* said that the hard men of Congress House would not endorse the plan which 'remains a rational vision for the future'. The *Observer* referred to the strike-torn country and said: 'There is, of course, a better way. It is set out in a pamphlet with that title, published last week by a group of General Council members on the personal initiative of Mr John Grant, a junior Employment Minister.'

The *Financial Times* said, 'the qualities of moderation and common sense which are evident in this document will certainly be needed.' The *Sun*'s industrial columnist, Peter McHugh, called it a remarkable document which outlined 'a brand new policy for getting around the yearly "dog eat dog" attitude to pay'. (He shrewdly noted the non-signatories, including David Basnett, the GMWU General Secretary, who he said had been forced to follow the path trodden by the TGWU's Moss Evans.) The *Daily Mirror*'s political editor, Terry Lancaster, said the document was responsible and intelligent. 'For once', he wrote, 'here is a document which lives up to its high-sounding title: "A Better Way".' There was plenty of other coverage, at home and abroad. American papers, which often carried stories about Britain's industrial ferment, now featured on their front pages this stand by the moderates.

In the Commons, at prime minister's question time, Jim Callaghan welcomed 'A Better Way': 'indeed', he told MPs, 'there must be for this country'. My involvement was an open secret so I wrote to Callaghan to explain my role. There was some media speculation that I had received an advance nod and wink from Jim, but that was nonsense. It was not his style to allow junior ministers a free run – as I had good reason to know from past experience. His reply, in a personal note, confirmed as much. He wrote: 'I was sorry your name came into it – but it is a good initiative. I would like to think that it can succeed before it is too late – for the unions, I mean!'

More than 12,000 copies of 'A Better Way' eventually went out, and we ended up making a profit – £400 – which we donated to charity. (The pamphlet has its echo in Labour's recent policy document, 'Labour's

Better Way for the 1990s'. It is a pity though that only the title and not the text has been cribbed from our earlier offering.)

The Concordat

It was February 1979. The government and the TUC agreed a 'concordat' to bring inflation down to 5 per cent in three years. It was born of desperation, a straw for government and unions alike to clutch at in the otherwise bleak combination of continuing strikes, grim weather and decidedly adverse public opinion polls.

A general election was imminent and Labour's chances seemed poor. The best that could be said for the concordat was that it helped to create a semblance of renewed awareness of economic realities. It opened the way to an overall economic assessment, involving government and industry. It was followed by the establishment of a new standing commission on pay comparability, chaired by Professor Hugh Clegg.

In the event, it was more or less irrelevant. The concordat, like 'A Better Way', was full of good intentions. But Joe Public needed a lot more than that. The excesses of Labour's industrial wing were all too fresh in people's minds, and Labour's political wing, inseparable from its trade union brothers, was lumbered with a shared responsibility for the winter's hardships. Moreover, the government and the party, riddled with doubt and deeply disheartened, had lost their bearings.

Labour's fall: Scottish devolution

Ostensibly, it was not the strikes that finally toppled the Callaghan government but parliamentary ferment over devolution for Scotland. The Scottish Nationalists, unable to secure the devolution deal which they demanded, put down a 'no confidence' motion. The Tories likewise registered a 'no confidence' motion. So on 28 March 1979, in a night of high drama in the Commons, Labour ministers attempted last-minute back-stage fixes to persuade MPs of minority parties to vote with them. The sick and ailing were ordered in to do their duty in the lobbies. (It was my wedding anniversary but we skipped the celebration.) The government was defeated by the narrowest possible margin – 311 votes to 310.

Labour was pitchforked into the general election. It was backs-to-the-wall for us, and we could have swapped our manifesto with the telephone directory. Who cared about our plans for the future? The devolution vote had triggered the contest, but devolution was of scant consequence at the hustings, outside of Scotland. Nothing could blot out the memories of the grim months which the nation had just endured. The Conservatives understandably made the most of it.

(The Prime Minister asked me to join his central campaign team. Once again I divided my time between my constituency and 10 Downing Street, handling the Callaghan newspaper articles. I drafted articles for the national dailies and Sundays, for provincial papers, trade union journals and for a variety of specialist publications aimed at anyone from church-goers to computer buffs. Jim Callaghan looked in occasionally, but, gratifyingly, never interfered.)

Labour's overall record was actually not so bad. Those governments from 1974 to 1979 had much to their credit. But the nation was in no mood to listen to explanations or even to apologies. There was no magic ingredient that could rescue us. Labour's union links were at the forefront of public consciousness and the unions were the subject of continuing scorn, even hatred. Labour, limp and exhausted, was tossed from power with its lowest share of the national poll since 1931. The Tories took 339 seats to our 269, and secured a majority of forty-three over all other parties. (I had another comfortable majority in Islington.)

It was the end of an era and the beginning of another. Government by corporation and consensus, maintained in varying degrees throughout the post-war period, was to be abandoned forthwith. A new ideology was on the march, and a new word was about to enter the British vocabulary. Thatcherism was with us. The unions were to pay a high price for their folly and inability to discipline themselves.

7

Breakaway Blues

For Labour there were dreary and depressing days ahead. The extended fratricidal inquest into what went wrong began, and charges and counter-charges abounded. The sad fact was that Labour had lost not only the general election, but also its own credibility. Doorstep doubtfuls and don't knows throughout the election campaign all talked of the winter of strikes and discontent. The unions got the blame, but Labour got the comeuppance. Jim Callaghan challenged the TUC to offer a viable alternative to his 5 per cent pay policy, even pleaded with them to do so, but it was to no avail.

Now Labour could only operate in the largely negative and reactive parliamentary role of government adversary. The Tories, cock-a-hoop, were understandably delighted at the disarray of their opponents. Thatcherism was on the march, and the economic and social face of Britain began to change drastically.

I called for a new agreement between Labour and the unions on incomes policy. My hopeful forecast, in the *Guardian*, was that 'the Labour Party will turn full circle on this issue, along with the unions'. This though, was a futuristic ripple in a tide of backward-looking condemnation by the Left of the villains of the parliamentary Labour Party and especially those of the Callaghan government. Some of these left-wing ne'er-do-wells managed to convince themselves that Labour lost because it lacked socialist conviction and policies. For others, the same conclusion was a cynical pretence which offered justification for their screaming aggression. They ignored the dramatic swing to the Right by the electorate. Yet these self-deluded nutters and their more malevolent extremist travelling companions in destruction gained increasing power within Labour's debilitated ranks. They created a breeding ground for an intolerance which found the party shedding disillusioned members like autumn leaves.

The unions had more pressing concerns of their own. They had placed themselves in the firing line. Margaret Thatcher informed the Commons that she had 'an absolute mandate' for her first industrial relations reform package. Her Employment Secretary, Jim Prior, proposed action on the closed shop, on postal ballots, on picketing. Initial reactions were mixed and somewhat confused. Tory-supporting newspapers were divided. The *Daily Telegraph* referred to 'Soft-pedal Tory union reform', while the *Daily Express* declared: 'Maggie Takes on Unions'. The *Sun* foresaw a replay of the 1971 confrontation and shouted: 'Here We Go Again'.

The proposals also undermined Labour's employment protection laws by easing restrictions which ministers claimed were costly and inhibited recruitment, particularly in small firms – in practice, the very places where many workers were exploited and in most need of protection.

At the first post-election Tory Party conference, Mrs Thatcher earned her ritual standing ovation from a captive (and captivated) audience with a blistering anti-union tirade. 'Millions of British workers go in fear of union power', she declared. 'The demand for this government to make changes is coming from the very people who experience this fear.' It was an exaggeration, but one which nevertheless contained more than a grain of truth. It was a populist sentiment which was well received beyond her own massed faithful. It was also an unmistakeable public directive to Jim Prior, whose instincts were more cautious and conciliatory, that he would not be allowed to backslide or wobble on the issue of industrial legislation.

Prior's Employment Bill

Prior's subsequent Bill showed little variation from the initial proposals. Union protestation got nowhere. Not that the Bill was all bad. Safeguards against coercive union recruitment, prevalent in parts of the printing industry, and the prevention of picket-line excesses, were much needed. There was a sweetener – state funds to help unions pay the cost of secret postal ballots. Prior claimed that his approach was 'fair-minded'. Eric Varley, Labour's employment spokesman, called it irrelevant to the nation's real problems. (I was appointed as one of Varley's deputies on employment and served on the Commons standing committee which dealt with legislation. I concentrated primarily on the clauses on individual rights, such as those making it more difficult for workers to win unfair dismissal cases at industrial tribunals and those repealing laws aimed at helping low-paid workers. These were areas where there was least justification for the government's position and I made the most of my plentiful ammunition. However, the government always had the votes and conceded next to nothing.)

Prior was hemmed in, as Thatcher dominated her Cabinet and Sir Geoffrey Howe, the Chancellor, and Sir Keith Joseph, the Industry Secretary, were unfailing in their support for union-bashing. They could always cite those who thought that it should all go much further. The right-wing Tory Monday Club published a series of draconian proposals:

(1) to give employers public funds to meet overheads during strikes;
(2) to eliminate social security for strikers;
(3) to compel unions to support strikers' families, with courts empowered to seize their funds if they failed to comply;
(4) to penalize workers by reducing pensions and redundancy payments according to the number and duration of strikes in which they took part.

The Monday Club document claimed further that 'Union power is the prerogative of the parasite.'

Alongside the attack on the unions, the government announced a nasty dose of doctrinal medicine. There would be massive cuts in aid for shipbuilding, steel and the regions, curbs on the National Enterprise Board's activities and British Airways, British Aerospace and the British National Oil Corporation would be sold off. Swingeing public spending cuts were the order of the day. Some of Labour's most ambitious projects were to be rapidly dismantled.

The government forged ahead with legislation and structural change, but its economic difficulties mounted. Minimum lending rate, mortgage rate and prices soared. Pay and price increases nudged towards 20 per cent. Cracks began to appear within the government. Prior earned the prime minister's open distaste for temporarily thwarting her most aggressive plans on picketing. John Biffen, Chief Secretary to the Treasury, spoke with brutal candour of 'unparalleled austerity' ahead and was angrily rebuffed by Thatcher.

The loss-making steel industry, already hard hit by redundancy, ran into an unexpected pay dispute. Customarily moderate employees rejected a pay offer seen as derisory when matched against steeply rising prices. Arthur Scargill, the miners' leader, flexed his muscles and waxed militant on the steelworkers' behalf. (I scoffed at his uninvited intervention, and told an Islington Trades Council meeting, well laced with left-wingers, that I deplored 'a well-heeled union official, not directly involved, advising workers to defy the law'. I added: 'Arthur Scargill should not seek to ride to power in the miners' union on the backs of striking steelworkers, grabbing a headline here and a TV fee there, as he goes.' Since I was a Labour Front-Bench spokesman I was widely reported.)

Howe's 1980 Budget chopped another £3,700 million from public spending, with a 1984 target date. There would be more huge cuts in aids to industry, in public works programmes and in benefits. Higher charges for rents, rates, fares, fuel, prescriptions and school meals would be accompanied by tax rises on drink, tobacco, petrol and car licences. Opposition Leader Jim Callaghan denounced the Budget as 'the most hopeless since the war and the meanest since 1931'.

There was no longer room to doubt the government's readiness to allow unemployment to climb substantially to combat inflation. The calculated spin-off was the adverse effect on the unions, on their bargaining capacity and their ability to resist. Unemployment hovered at around 1,500,000 and the more gloomy economists predicted 3,500,000 out of work by 1985. Tory MPs worried that recession would not be conquered before they next faced the electorate, but Thatcher was undeterred. In the Commons, Howe produced a combination of blatant evasion and classic gobbledegook when he was pressed about the mounting jobless total. His extraordinary response was that 'the Conservative Party is dedicated to the restoration of nearer to full employment.' (Presumably, that historic declaration remains the Tory policy position.)

Prior's Bill progressed through the Commons and the Lords. There was no disposition by Labour MPs to spin it out by futile late-night filibusters, either in committee or on the floor of the House, as we had done back in 1971 during Heath's Industrial Relations Bill. Varley got some left-wing criticism for not fighting hard enough, but there was no serious union pressure. The unions now had all the spark of a dud battery. The TUC tried to organize a Day of Action against Prior's Bill – a tactic openly opposed by Frank Chapple and the EETPU as 'untimely and unwise'. The action was a flop, and Chapple was chastized by the TUC General Council for being right.

There was a plethora of complaints from Labour about the Bill's shoddy draftsmanship and the loopholes open to be exploited by militant unionists or rogue employers. Labour lawyers tabled more than 400 amendments in the Lords, and claimed that the legislation would prove to be more disruptive than Heath's Act. But Prior argued that the Heath laws proved 'completely unworkable' and that he had learned from those mistakes. The Bill completed its parliamentary passage.

The government plunged on with a further avalanche of controversial measures. The education budget was cut; the link between pensions and the retail price index was severed; a Bill paved the way for private bus operators; council house sales and council rent rises were enforced; short-term benefits were reduced, the earnings-related supplement was phased out and benefits to strikers' families were axed. It was proper for the government to implement its election pledges, but there was now an unseemly haste to get the dirty work out of the way well before the next election. The result was a good deal of hastily drafted and ill-considered legislation.

Labour's former deputy leader, Roy Jenkins, returned from his Brussels role as President of the European Commission to begin his campaign to establish a new third force in British politics. His re-entry to the political scene was premature, but Labour foolishly shunned his underlying message – that unless the middle ground was won, then there would be no prospect of lasting power.

The burgeoning Left, supremely arrogant, blindly ignored the wishes of the ordinary citizen, not merely those in suburbia, but also those on the council estates and the shop-floor. Labour headed towards further disaster by allowing itself to be presented as extreme and, worse still, by being so. The long-term political wilderness loomed unless the party could reconcile the differences between democratic socialist aspirations and the pragmatism and self-interest of the average voter.

Several of Labour's senior figures sought to rekindle the incomes policy argument, though their support was mostly tentative and qualified. David Owen, the former Foreign Secretary, sent me a draft speech for my comments. I urged him to include redistribution since incomes policy had to be 'sold' on grounds of equity, not power. I said that it was important to allow variations within the criteria to take account of issues like low pay. (He was sceptical then and has since become increasingly disenchanted with any form of centralized intervention in wage bargaining.) Roy Hattersley also sent me a draft speech, warning of the unfortunate consequences if Labour rejected incomes policy. I pointed out to him that we had already done so.

I kept up my own efforts in a series of speeches. I accused the party's National Executive Committee of deliberately avoiding the question of incomes policy – 'a virtually unmentionable phrase'. I said: 'If the unions understandably deny co-operation on pay to a Tory government that offers them no return, will they also deny it to a Labour government trying to achieve a different kind of society?'

'Labour First'

I was one of those Labour MPs not formally aligned with either the right-wing Manifesto Group or its rival left-wing Tribune Group. Groups spelled dissension, and membership of the party was enough. However, along with two parliamentary friends, Brynmor John and Terry Davis, I was deeply unhappy with the faction fighting which now bedevilled the parliamentary party as well as the party beyond.

We sounded out other like-minded MPs and set up a new moderate grouping to try to counter the polarization of the party at Westminster and to foster 'an improved spirit of tolerance'. We called ourselves 'Labour First'.

There was resentment that elections for the Shadow Cabinet were conducted on the basis of slates of candidates drawn up by the existing two conflicting groups. There was little chance for those in the middle, and the Shadow Cabinet was unrepresentative. We advanced our own slate. Our early meetings were well attended. Brynmor was elected chairman and I was vice-chairman. Our steering committee included several of the current Labour front bench: Sir Peter Archer, David Clark, George Foulkes.

Labour had established a special commission of inquiry to consider constitutional changes to the party structure and procedures. Instead of reform to carry us forward, the commission pressed the self-destruct button. There was a 'summit' conference with the unions. The awful upshot was proposals for: the removal from Labour MPs of their exclusive right to choose the party leader (a change reluctantly and foolishly endorsed by Jim Callaghan); compulsory re-selection of sitting MPs; stripping the parliamentary leadership of its right to have the final word in drawing up the election manifesto with this power passing to the National Executive Committee. It was a corrosive formula.

The calamitous commission's findings overshadowed the party's

1980 conference, an ugly, introverted affair, which at times degenerated into a maniacal hullabaloo, devoid of fraternity or comradeship. (Nor were the nation's troubles of much concern.) Ill-thought-out emotive decisions were made in an unpleasant atmosphere of booing, hissing and slow handclaps. There were personal slanging matches, and ill-tempered meetings of the National Executive Committee, copiously reported via leaks, to our public discomfort and embarrassment. The proposed constitutional package would be dealt with at a special conference to be held at Wembley early in 1981. That delay guaranteed further months of wolfish snarling and snapping.

By contrast, that year's Tory conference was full of arid complacency and smug self-congratulation. The economic storm signals were plain to see but Mrs Thatcher capitalized unscrupulously on Labour's disarray. 'You turn if you want to – the lady's not for turning', she pronounced, to the adulation of her flock.

Labour's internal power struggle

Jim Callaghan's long innings was over. He stood down from the party leadership. Once Labour had lost the election everyone knew it was only a matter of how long he would sit things out. He had held all the great offices of state – Chancellor of the Exchequer, Foreign Secretary, Home Secretary – before his premiership. Like Harold Wilson, Jim was a canny and skilled political in-fighter. He was a quality performer on the party platform or at the parliamentary despatch box. Tall, grey-haired, slightly stoop-shouldered, he commanded a stature which his unremarkable balance sheet in office hardly justified. At 10 Downing Street he had managed to exude an air of calm self-confidence and stern authority while presiding over a crumbling political edifice. His lame refusal to take on the Ford Motor Company and the unions to sustain his pay policy had been a critical failure. Now he was unable to prevent Labour's constitutional monstrosities – changes which led directly to the founding of the Social Democrats. Perhaps though, he was really Unlucky Jim, pitchforked into No. 10 at a time when crisis was pre-ordained, was unavoidable. He did his best to keep Labour's show on the road, whatever his mistakes.

Labour was plunged into a period of ever more vicious combat. The succession to Callaghan was critical, fateful, in the party's struggle for renewed credibility and hence for survival. Foot and Healey were now direct rivals.

Foot v. Healey

Michael Foot was the Left's natural choice as leader. He had refrained from rocking the boat while in government, despite his rebellious character. His talent though, was for extravagant conference rhetoric, for uplifting platform oratory, not for decision-taking. He was not so muddled, gabby or intellectual as was commonly perceived. But his apparent strengths and failings were allied to a political past of left-wing protest which made him an electoral liability. Public sightings of this shop-soiled old-timer were more cost-effective for the Tories than any conventional advertising they might devise.

Denis Healey was the clear contender from the Right. Denis had his own intellectual qualities, mostly cloaked by a bruising and cheerfully combative spirit which occasionally spilled over into bullying. His tough-guy capers were anathema to his left-wing adversaries. There were times too, when he seemed to turn expediency into an art form. He had moved imperturbably from a pro- to an anti-EEC stance. His switch reflected the anti-Marketry among many of Labour's moderates whose support he thought he might need sometime. He knew he would never lose the more ardent pro-Marketeers in a battle with the Left because they had nowhere else to go.

The Hard Left ran an intimidatory campaign to stop Healey. They tried to prevent the parliamentary party from holding an immediate leadership election so that it could be held later under the proposed new rules which they hoped that the forthcoming special conference would endorse. I was among sixty-two Labour MPs who openly declared that the election should go ahead. We were denounced by the Left and *Tribune*, the left-wing weekly, suggested that I would be censured by my local constituency party. (Instead, my people decisively rejected any delay. The Left's influence in Central Islington was growing, but was not yet a serious threat.)

I lobbied for Healey, as I had no doubt that Foot would be a disastrous choice. Shortly before the votes were cast I went to Australia as part of a Commonwealth Parliamentary Association delegation. I gave my proxy vote to Brynmor John and asked him to stick with Healey right through, though if Healey was inexplicably not in the final ballot – 'through falling under a bus' – to use my vote for Peter Shore, another of the candidates. I was still in Australia when the shock news came through that Foot had won. It was an appalling and deeply depressing outcome.

Intimidation on the part of the Left had worked. Labour MPs looked apprehensively over their shoulders at pending re-selection. Irresponsibly, they shied away from a pro-Healey decision which might bring a backlash against them in the many constituencies where the Left was riding high. Even more irresponsible and cynical was the behaviour of a handful of right-wingers who voted for Foot in the belief that it would hasten the final bust-up between Labour's warring factions and would lead to the establishment of a new moderate centre party of the kind Roy Jenkins peddled. Their analysis of the ultimate effect of Foot's victory turned out to be correct, but their action in the ballot, subsequently admitted in one or two cases, was an exercise in political prostitution.

Foot's election solved nothing. Labour's internal power struggle intensified. Benn now had a worse relationship with his old ally, Foot, than he had had with the departed Jim Callaghan. Denis Healey secured the deputy leadership. The Shadow Cabinet recommended to the parliamentary party that the principle of an electoral college to choose the leader and deputy leader should be conceded at the special conference, provided that MPs received 50 per cent of the college votes. Sixteen of us rebelled and tabled an unsuccessful amendment declining to accept the college as legitimate and democratic in the absence of assurances that the National Executive Committee would recommend that individual constituency parties should vote by postal ballot of their paid-up members and that the affiliated unions should prevent non-Labour members from influencing their votes within the college.

The special conference at Wembley was a resounding victory for the Bennite Rank-and-File Mobilizing Committee. The Left had burrowed feverishly within the unions, and had ensnared enough block votes to produce an electoral college which gave the unions 40 per cent of the votes, with 30 per cent each for MPs and the constituencies.

There was a prompt reaction by 150 Labour MPs who issued a statement describing the college voting formula as a mistake that should be quickly rectified. Our statement also condemned proposals to bind MPs to specific policy commitments through loyalty oaths – another dangerous idea that was an integral part of the Left platform.

The SDP: the Limehouse Declaration

Such limited reprisals were not enough for Shirley Williams, David Owen and Bill Rodgers, all former Cabinet ministers. They joined with Roy Jenkins to form the Gang of Four and set up the Council for Social

Democracy. They issued the Limehouse Declaration – a call to 'all those who are committed to the values, principles and policies of social democracy'. Irreconcileable differences were now institutionalized. It was not long before the quartet broke away from Labour and founded the Social Democratic Party. Jenkins and Shirley Williams (who had lost her Commons seat) were not MPs, but nine other MPs stood alongside Owen and Rodgers as the new party was launched.

It was hard to attend to parliamentary matters or to the interests of constituents against the fast-changing bubbling Labour domestic scene. The Tories had their own alarms as rumour implied an exodus of Tory 'wets' to the SDP, but in the event only one Tory MP eventually defected.

Those destructive Wembley conference decisions hung like a huge black cloud over the demoralized parliamentary Labour Party. The independence of Labour MPs was severely curtailed by them and many of us believed that the party's hopes of regaining power in the foreseeable future had vanished. Even younger MPs considered that they were unlikely to see another Labour government during their political lifetimes. Massive hurdles had now to be cleared for Labour to win another election. Those hurdles included: the Tories' seventy-seat Commons majority over Labour; likely gains to the Tories of about twenty seats through pending boundary changes; the probability of Labour MPs, de-selected under the new mandatory process, standing against official Labour candidates; and a gift-wrapped propaganda package – in the shape of Mr Benn – for the Tories to use on the doorstep to frighten voters. Most importantly, there was the dramatic effect on the electorate of the new SDP and its alliance with the Liberals.

The Shadow Cabinet fudged rather than fought the Left. Its reward was to see the parliamentary party trampled underfoot. Desertion was anathema for most MPs. Yet there could be no collective conscience. Cries of 'treachery' or 'good riddance' were futile, solved nothing and ignored the pain and the sincerity of those concerned as they stumbled, all too slowly, to their verdict. (I was soon to experience first-hand that very pain.)

Labour Solidarity

I played a leading role in Labour Solidarity, set up by a meeting of more than a hundred MPs who sought to promote party unity, but were primarily concerned to stop unrepresentative and extremist minorities

106

from gaining further ground. The group's base was the Commons but we aimed to establish local groups in a bid to counter the Left stranglehold that was already to be found in areas of local government. We were out to forge trade union links, too, and my contacts proved useful. I was elected to Solidarity's steering committee and took responsibility for overseeing a monthly newsletter, edited by the journalist-peer John Bevan (Lord Ardwick). The group's co-chairmen were Roy Hattersley and Peter Shore.

Labour Solidarity gave temporary hope to those moderate MPs who refused to become part of the steady trickle of defection to the mushrooming SDP. Yet Solidarity's in-built handicaps were considerable. It sought to attract the soft Left. Neil Kinnock, still uncertain where his best friends and prospects lay, was unsuccessfully wooed. MPs such as Frank Field and Martin O'Neill climbed aboard, but their uneasy presence induced the committee to water down its challenge.

Tony Benn announced that he would contest the deputy leadership. Solidarity declared itself for the existing Foot–Healey duo, and I penned a forthright pro-Healey leading article for our newsletter. Our arrangement was that I needed the approval of the co-chairmen for contentious pieces which committed Solidarity. That was fair enough. Hattersley agreed with the pro-Healey article, as did a committee meeting. Shore, however, was away, and returned just in time to use his veto, much to my disgust. I had a heated argument with him. In deadlock, we recalled the committee to decide. Shore seemed to me to be anxious to keep flexibility in preparation for his own future leadership bid. That could bring him into conflict with Healey over moderate support and he did not want Solidarity indelibly written onto a Healey ticket. We had a wrangle inside the committee, but the majority favoured a toned-down version of the article. (Another example of Solidarity feebleness was a decision not to take up an offer to use the EETPU's computer because it was used previously by the right-wing group, Campaign for Labour Victory. The EETPU, which sponsored me, was unpopular within the party and a good many of the CLV leaders were now with the SDP. But the EETPU was affiliated to Labour, which gladly took its cash. The proposed computer boycott was, I protested, 'carrying sensitivity and hypocrisy to pretty extraordinary heights'.) These were the kind of weaknesses which eventually convinced me that Labour's moderates lacked the stamina and bottle to win the fight.

The Left had secured so much that they perversely urged the party to accept the new constitutional position and to concentrate on attacking the Tories – a bare-faced posture which contrasted sharply with their out-of-hand rejection of unity calls prior to the previous October's conference shambles. Their bellicose pledge then was to continue the civil war until they won outright victory, that is, reforms on their unyielding terms.

The Bennite allies – the Rank-and-File Mobilizing Committee, Militant, the Labour Co-ordinating Committee and the Socialist Campaign for Labour Party Democracy – were an unrelenting chain gang which gave their first loyalty not to the Labour Party but to their own narrow factions. They incessantly peddled the myth of betrayal by the last Labour government. They were Labour's real enemies and they had supporters who drew their government salaries when the party held office.

They maintained their offensive to gain further control. They manœuvred to give Labour's National Executive Committee the whip hand in deciding a manifesto which a Labour government, backed by Labour MPs, would have to implement. Parliamentary democracy would have been jeopardized if proposals had gone ahead to make MPs responsible, not to the British public, but to an unrepresentative party caucus.

The Social Democrats were up and running, ever harder. Roy Jenkins missed by a whisker in a by-election attempt to capture the once rock-solid Labour seat at Warrington. Even the left-wing Doug Hoyle, who squeaked home, declared: 'Tony Benn was the issue. Once that was raised the door was closed on you.' Those who glibly blamed a hostile media for the humiliation because of a supposed fear of a Benn-led Labour Party, should have asked which politician the Tories, the Liberals, and especially the Social Democrats, would have most liked to see leading Labour at the next general election. What the media reflected during the Warrington campaign, in particular, was a trend back towards a desire for consensus politics. Ordinary voters were bewildered by and deeply suspicious of those who constantly preached their own ideologies and lectured others on what was good for them.

Too many Labour activists believed that it was better to renounce power than to respond to what the public wanted and might accept. Too many of them believed that Britain brimmed with a great untapped demand for huge bucketsful of socialism. They talked to each other. They were deaf to the talk in the pubs and clubs, on the shopfloor, in the offices. They were condescending about unbelievers and scorned sensible compromise. They forced Labour to once again choose whether it should be a party of government or a party of protest, a dilemma which Harold Wilson optimistically thought he had had resolved for good back in the mid-sixties. Now the growing strength of the Hard Left made the prospect of another Labour government increasingly unlikely.

Benn argued, sanctimoniously but quite persuasively, for a contest for the deputy leadership. 'Regular elections', he said, 'are the lifeblood of democracy.' The newly established 'democratic machinery' should now be used. It was an indication of his double standards, extolling the virtues of the mock democracy which now prevailed. The Left though, was in the ascendancy. From the outside, looking in, it looked reasonable enough to give their standard-bearer a chance to prove that Labour was now ruled by an unrepresentative right-wing clique. (Some standard-bearer! Some democracy!) Labour needed another heavy-weight election scrap like a hole in the head.

Tories v. unions: Tebbit takes over

Labour was in ferment and so too were its union kin. The Tories were out to make the most of it, and the pressure was on for a fresh package of trade union reform. There had been industrial peace since Prior's 1980 Employment Act. No one believed that the legislation, still largely untested, was responsible, it was rather the threat of unemployment that kept workers quiescent.

Ministers knew that the unions were in no condition to take them on. The miners had faced Mrs Thatcher out and provided the unions with a brief respite. Pit closure plans provoked a miners' strike vote. Mrs Thatcher avoided confrontation by announcing more public money for the coal industry and a withdrawal of the closure programme. But unemployment saw 1,000,000 union members disappear in two years and the screw still turned. The biggest union, the Transport and General Workers', lost 300,000 members and its annual income slumped by more than £5 million. The trade unions' voice became a whimper. The government governed and ignored them. Their fierce vocal opposition to new laws was exposed as hot air.

Mrs Thatcher and her anti-union Cabinet hawks reckoned that there could be no better climate in which to hit harder than ever at Labour's paymasters and to do them permanent damage. Prior produced a Green Paper with fresh proposals. It was an open secret that he did not want to trample on the unions, but rather wished to allow his earlier reforms to bed down. His so-called step-by-step approach was not enough for a prime minister determined to arraign the unions as her necessary scapegoats for the nation's ills.

Jim Prior's constant disagreements with Margaret Thatcher broke into the open again. He still forecast 3,000,000 out of work and was crudely slapped down by her in the Commons. She proclaimed 'clear signs that the worst of the recession is over'. Their hostilities could not go on – and indeed didn't. Prior was shuffled off to Northern Ireland and the aggressive and abrasive Industry Minister, Norman Tebbit, arrived at the Department of Employment with an unmistakeable mission to put the boot into the unions.

The TUC's Len Murray said: 'With Conservative economic policy in ruins, further legislation may be one way of trying to keep the party faithful happy.' The political case for forcing the pace of reform was overwhelmingly attractive to Tory hardliners and certainly to the Prime Minister. It was not Prior's style, but it was tailor-made for Tebbit. Tebbit toughened up Prior's proposals with a Bill that included a variety of controversial measures. He tackled the closed shop – but with some caution, undermining but not banning it. He lifted much of the immunity from legal action for damages which unions hitherto enjoyed in so-called 'trades disputes'. Surprisingly, he failed to remove immunity for strikes called without a ballot.

Brighton 1981

At what was to be my last Labour Party conference, the incomes policy issue was squeezed back onto the agenda through motions from the NUR, the steelworkers and the communications workers. Their view was that if the next Labour government was to go for necessary economic expansion without risking the all-too-familiar inflationary spiral in which the poor are hit first and hardest, an incomes policy remained of crucial importance. Their motions got nowhere.

Our pre-conference Sunday morning Solidarity fringe meeting was packed to hear Jim Callaghan, Peter Shore, Roy Hattersley and a bevy of sympathetic union leaders. Healey arrived from a divisive National Executive Committee meeting to a hero's welcome. It was heady stuff, and it seemed certain that Healey would confound Tony Benn and would be elected deputy leader with a fair-sized majority.

In the event, Healey's victory margin was wafer thin. TGWU leaders had proclaimed their support for the Foot–Healey ticket but the union's dubious voting behaviour was maintained right to the end. Its Brighton conference delegation swung the union's block vote behind Benn. Healey could only scrape up 20 per cent support from the militant constituencies. But the National Union of Public Employees unexpectedly backed him and a number of Tribunite MPs, disgusted at the discord caused by Benn's antics, abstained.

Benn was helped by the intimidation factor. MPs' votes were on the record, and Left-dominated local parties were due to re-select. Enough MPs – just enough – stood firm, but revenge was openly talked of.

What the contest highlighted above all, was the fiasco of the diverse voting methods used by the unions to decide on their chosen candidate. A few balloted their members. Some were committed by their annual conferences. Others imposed executive rulings in the traditional smoke-filled rooms. Still, Healey was home and dry, and the moderates could celebrate.

The Bennites had appeared to be *en route* to a hat-trick of successes. Mandatory re-selection one year. The electoral college the next. Now control of the election manifesto was about to pass to an uninhibited and leftish National Executive Committee. The conference voted narrowly for this switch – in principle. Foot argued strongly against the change, but journalists started to write their 'Foot humiliated' stories and the hardliners were cock-a-hoop. But Labour's conference, unpredictable as ever, failed to amend the constitution to put the principle into practice. The full implications of the earlier vote and the damage it could do to Labour's election chances, began to sink in. Block votes began to shift and there was a much-needed reprieve.

There was good news too, from the National Executive Committee elections. Eric Varley ousted the left-wing Norman Atkinson from the treasurership. A vicious hardline campaign to dispose of soft lefties Neil Kinnock and Joan Lestor, abstainers in the Healey–Benn vote, was rebuffed. The moderates gained two places in the trade union section and three seats in the women's section. The Left had suffered a sizeable reverse.

Superficially, two years of turmoil seemed to be ending in a return to moderation, and on the face of it the Bennites looked vulnerable. The fightback seemed to be paying dividends. What, though, was the reality? The moderates had held the line, however dodgily, over control of the manifesto but there was no hope of reversing the deplorable decisions for mandatory re-selection and for the electoral college. The National Executive Committee had 'swung to the Right' but such terms were strictly relative. Some of those who now attracted moderate

111

support were well to the Left not long before and their allegiance could shift again in expedient fashion. Ironically, Healey's win over Benn owed much to the block votes of unions that failed to consult their members, even though a majority of ordinary trade unionists would have almost certainly backed Healey in a ballot.

If the constitution remained an unacceptable mess, so did policy. Labour had lurched unequivocally into the unilateral nuclear disarmament camp. Labour was anti-Market. Whatever the scepticism about the European ideal, a British withdrawal meant grave and far-reaching economic, social and political consequences. It was unthinkable. Labour's predominant 'little Englanders' were a liability to the party and to the nation. Incomes policy and the trade union question were a graveyard of lost hopes. Michael Foot promised a more fruitful relationship with the unions under another Labour government. Contrast that with the conference which began with an unconditional rejection of moves to construct anew an agreed and effective incomes policy.

All this and Michael Foot, too. He had a fair conference, probably the most successful week of his 11-months leadership. But that said little. It would take far more than Brighton to erase the public image of vacillation, weakness, irrelevancy and bottled-up left-wing beliefs. Trouble was, that public perception was broadly correct.

Islington topped it all up for me. It was always a political battleground. Now it produced more bile and bitterness than ever before. The problems were far from insurmountable, but the future looked bleak. True, the extremists were not in control, but decent people were clinging on to membership with no enthusiasm and often only because of my personal pleas. It couldn't last. Nor did Labour deserve that it should. I no longer believed in the party that I loved. I was living in a make-believe world, living a lie and had to quit. It was by far the most anguished and traumatic decision of my political existence, perhaps of any that I have had to take.

There are those who joyously leaped from Labour to the SDP and claimed that a great weight had been lifted from them. That was not my experience. After all, only a week or two earlier I was determined to stay and struggle on, had even influenced waverers to do just that (as they later told me). My painful self-analysis revealed just how far out of step I was with the overwhelming majority of those who had seized our levers of power, who were really in charge. 'My party, right or wrong' is both unprincipled and undemocratic. Loyalty and sentiment are admirable qualities but loyalty can be grossly misguided, even false, and sentiment blurs sound judgement and truth.)

The unions were rapidly losing their industrial strength. Inside the Labour Party, however, they continued to dominate through their block votes at the conference and to use those votes to back policies that ensured that Labour would revert to being a party of protest, not a potential party of government.

8

Tebbit Raises the Tempo

The TUC was outraged by the industrial relations reform proposals produced by Norman Tebbit late in 1981 and it carried on sustained and indiscriminate resistance to them.

The unions were no real match for the new Employment Minister whose scheme carefully avoided compulsion and the risk of creating union martyrs. Tebbit shrewdly concentrated on weakening and diminishing the so-called privileges which legal immunity had given to the unions in the past. He claimed that he was no 'union basher' and aggressively contrasted his 'desirable' reforms with the behaviour of those in the unions who bashed 'the old, the sick, the unemployed, the disabled' in the Winter of Discontent.

There were two key areas of change in what he proposed. The first significantly increased compensation for those dismissed because of a closed shop so that workers could, in effect, seek compensation from the union concerned in addition to their former employer. Contracts which specified union-only labour were nullified and immunity was removed from those organizing industrial action to back the closed shop.

Secondly, Tebbit opened up the unions themselves to damages if they committed unlawful acts except in 'pursuit or furtherance' of a 'trades dispute' and for unlawful secondary picketing and attempts to enforce union membership. He underpinned that change by narrowing the definition of a 'trades dispute' to effectively outlaw 'political' strikes (for instance, against the government) and strikes about matters outside the country.

The unions saw these as hammer blows at their ability to mount effective industrial action, a view that was not without justification. TUC opposition to Tebbit's package built up to a crescendo and to a

TUC conference decision to fight the new laws first and foremost 'industrially and not in the courts'. That would put the unions outside the law and make them participants in illegal action. It was the TUC at its most emotive, muddle-headed and dangerously vulnerable. It ignored the government's democratic mandate to curb union power. It ignored too, opinion polls which showed clearly enough that the public, and union members too, favoured more union reform laws. It was a major fillip for Tebbit. Once again, the TUC had brought itself into public disrepute to the advantage of the Conservative government. Moreover, it was defiance by the union leadership that was sparsely supported at the grass-roots and, inevitably, it fizzled out.

(Meanwhile, I had left the Labour Party. In a Commons speech explaining my decision, I was highly critical of Foot's leadership – his continued attempts to appease the unappeasable – and of the growing intolerance and intimidation within the party. Soon after that I joined the SDP, the twenty-third Labour MP to do so. Labour's Hard Left had long claimed that right-wingers who could not accept the new Left-imposed policies should get out. Now they branded every fresh defection as treachery while privately chortling as their moderate opponents in the party dwindled.)

I quickly became the SDP's parliamentary spokesman on employment (and later on industry). I was elected as Chairman of the newly formed Association of Social Democratic Trade Unionists.

Tebbit's Bill rapidly involved me in a fierce controversy within the SDP. I had condemned his proposals from the Labour benches, recognizing that, though there were useful aspects to the proposals, the overall package would not improve industrial relations, nor indeed was that its prime purpose. I could not contrive a sudden expedient change of heart now that I was with the SDP. The SDP itself hoped to establish informal union links, but private sympathy among leading trade unionists had yet to be translated into worthwhile open support. We could not be seen to side with Tebbit, or we would earn an unequivocal anti-union tag.

Tebbit had not changed his spots since his behaviour as a backbench MP earned him his Chingford skinhead title. He inherited much of his legislative portfolio from Jim Prior. It could have been far tougher, but Tebbit, despite his abrasive reputation, was realistic about how much he should pack into a single Bill. Even so, he spoke provocatively about 'neutering' union practices. The left-wing Alan Sapper, cine technicians' union leader and the then TUC Chairman, called the Bill a declaration of war on the working class which would 'virtually destroy the trade union movement if it is not resisted'. This was nonsense – as most people realized. Yet even moderates like Terry Duffy, Bill Sirs and David Basnett huffed and puffed, and hinted at deliberate law-breaking.

Tebbit was delighted with all this. He knew that any effective TUC action was a non-runner. The more fuss the unpopular unions made, the more public sympathy and support he would receive. (Tebbit is a wily bird for whom I had, and have, considerable respect. He bounced back with vigour after the devastating effect of the IRA's Brighton bomb wickedness which so tragically crippled his wife. Some of his right-wing views were savagely marketed to attract maximum attention, but he had a grassroots understanding which is rare among Tory politicians and was quite different to Enoch Powell's superimposed professorial brand of populism. Behind the scenes, Tebbit was unstuffy and amusing, but this did not prevent me from describing him in the Commons as 'the Prime Minister's pet piranha' – a phrase which tickled the fancies of the parliamentary sketch-writers.)

The SDP and the unions

Inside the SDP's group of MPs, we had a lengthy and irascible debate about Tebbit's Bill. Shirley Williams was missing, but she had let it be known that she was unhappy at the prospect of supporting it. There was a three-way split among our MPs which was reflected in the division on the Bill's second reading. Owen and Rodgers took the largest group into the 'aye' lobby, together with a vacillating Shirley Williams. As the SDP's employment spokesman, I was seen as the ringleader of the rebellious five who voted 'No'. There was one deliberate abstention and several of our doubters were conveniently 'paired' with absent MPs from other parties.

Like the unions, we had botched it. Not surprisingly, we were ridiculed by the Tories, Labour and the media. We could hardly complain, as we had failed to get our act together on our first major parliamentary test.

Bill Rodgers spoke for us in the debate. I stayed silent, rather than cause further embarrassment by putting a contrary view on the floor of the House. Our official line was that we would review our position after the Bill had been through the committee stage. Our vote at the third reading would depend on what improvements had been made.

There were no improvements. I saw no way of changing my vote, without appearing hypocritical. I told a meeting of our MPs that unity on that basis would be seen to be spurious. 'We would', I said, 'be vote-cadging and playing to excess the party games which we are supposed to deplore.' The SDP MPs agreed to abstain, except for me. It was an odd experience, playing a lone hand and back in the lobby, crowded with Labour MPs.

The SDP was in the process of developing its own industrial relations plans, and I was deeply involved. We sought to extend the use of secret ballots in union elections more comprehensively than the government proposed, to reopen the issue of industrial democracy and to challenge Labour's financial bonds with the unions. The unions attacked us over that pro-Tory second reading vote on Tebbit's Bill. I retorted that 'it's a pity that union leaders did not discuss this with us'. That brought a *Guardian* leading article which broadly agreed with me, but added:

Mr Grant, an able junior minister at Employment in the 1970s, was very much of the social contract/incomes policy school of pragmatic socialism. . . . Almost despite themselves, the Social Democrats are evolving a radical, reformist stance on industrial relations which could prove seductive to union members as well as to more natural Conservative voters. . . . But Mr Grant would be dangerously mistaken if he believed that the Barons of Congress House are in the market for anything half as radical.

I could not dispute that somewhat depressing assessment of the union scene.

(I was regrettably obliged to sever my own link as a sponsored EETPU MP. Had I not done so, the Labour-affiliated union would have needed to act. I wrote to Frank Chapple, explaining my reasons for leaving Labour and joining the SDP. The union's Executive Council issued a statement to say that the main policy and constitutional issues which led to my departure were matters where my position was closely in line with that of the union which shared my concern 'at the growth of extremism in the Labour Party'. The statement regretted my decision to leave, praised my service to Labour, to the unions and to the EETPU and suggested that I would remain 'entirely sympathetic to that which is best in the British trade union movement'.

What I didn't know at the time was that there was a serious discussion on the Executive Council about holding a membership referendum on whether or not to stay affiliated to Labour. There was little doubt that the members at that time would have balloted to disaffiliate. The danger was only averted by Frank Chapple's warning that such an outcome would split the union and play into the hands of the Communists and other extremists within its ranks. I remained a member of the union and, although I didn't know it then, was soon to be more involved with it than ever.)

A few months earlier I had taken over from John Cartwright, MP, as parliamentary consultant to the Banking, Insurance and Finance Union, not Labour-affiliated, but committed to having one MP adviser from the government benches and one from the official Opposition. Cartwright's move to the SDP left a gap which I filled. Now I had followed suit and could only apologize to BIFU for my short stay. I was swiftly invited to adopt a similar role for the First Division Association, another non-Labour union which represents senior civil servants. The FDA had Tory and Labour advisers. Now that the SDP/Liberal Alliance was an established political force, it wanted one of us. Moreover, there was a good deal of support for the Alliance within the Association, including its Executive Council, probably reflecting the consensus approach favoured by many civil servants and traditionally the basis of Whitehall ideology.

Incomes policy

The SDP should have been the party of incomes policy and thus distinctive from both the Tories and Labour. Distinctive too, from the TUC, which continued to cling to the totem pole of free collective bargaining. Unemployment topped three million, yet the unions still shunned any promise to co-operate in an incomes policy, even under Labour.

My suspicion about the SDP was that an incomes policy might lose out in any attempt to reconcile it with the market economy which figured so large in the party's thinking. If so, an incomes policy could vanish from the agenda. When the conference was over, I fired a warning shot in *The Times*: 'If the Social Democrats, in particular, go cool on incomes policy, then a good many of those who joined in good faith will have been seriously misled.'

The party's economic policy committee pressed on with its own incomes policy discussions. There were a range of views, from enthusiasts like me who reckoned that it was vital if we were to achieve economic expansion without crippling inflation, to those whose defence of it resembled Maurice Chevalier's description of old age – better than the only alternative.

Once we got down to detail it became increasingly problematical. We knew that the Liberals favoured a statutory policy and it was necessary to take their views on board. Roy Jenkins, now the SDP's leader and back in the Commons, was in broad agreement with them, but the SDP's own academics were divided. Professor Richard Layard urged a tax on high wage settlements, which Jenkins supported. Professor Joan Mitchell opposed this and was close to the kind of policy I had outlined in my pamphlet 'A Better Way'. Professor James Meade, Nobel prizewinner and the committee's guru, opted for tough curbs on wage bargaining power through arbitration, all linked to the direct promotion of employment. Lord Roberthall, another distinguished economist, who claimed to be the earliest advocate in the Treasury for incomes policy, and the ex-Treasury Minister Dick Taverne, advanced their ideas.

I chipped in with a paper in which I sought to reconcile the wage inflation tax with a more traditional prices and incomes policy. I concluded that the two couldn't operate in tandem. I backed a largely voluntary policy and said: 'The wage inflation tax is somewhat unambitious and offers across-the-board restraint while making no attack on wage-bargaining inadequacies. It seems to me to be settling for second-best and should therefore be our fallback position.' That way, I argued, a largely voluntary carrot would be offered but the compulsory stick would be a quite visible alternative.

The SDP groped for a way forward, for a solution to the seemingly insoluble. The Conservative government had its own covert incomes policy. It was called unemployment, and was a crude, unjust and arguably self-defeating policy for a nation in desperate need of restored economic fortune. Labour's position was best summarized by the NUR's Sid Weighell, who told his members that Labour's proposals for rigorous price controls, with no check on wages, 'is a prescription for bankruptcies, closures and unemployment on an even more gigantic scale than hitherto . . . yet that is precisely the state of the party's counter-inflation policy at the present time'. Labour had abandoned incomes policy and the few, such as Sid Weighell, who recognized this as a grievous error, got no thanks for doing so.

Labour's slide continued. Foot mildly dismissed the Militant Tendency as a 'pestilential nuisance' and refused to demand their expulsion from the Party. Labour's broad church crumbled around him but he scoffed at the SDP as 'an idle threat'. The Trots worked away at their hit list, aimed at ousting good Labour MPs who would not conform to the new Left zealots who ruled in so many constituencies. Benn would not disown them. More and more Labour MPs who had backed Foot against Healey, as a potential unifier, now recognized privately that unity had given way to sell-out.

The NUM: Arthur Scargill

The government's flagging popularity had been bolstered by the so-called 'Falklands Factor'. Margaret Thatcher made the most of the Union Jack and the nation rallied behind it, to Conservative advantage. Soon after that the government acquired another huge bonus, as Arthur Scargill swaggered once more into the limelight.

Scargill's militant supporters had attacked his predecessor at the NUM, Joe Gormley. Joe bowed out with a message to the miners to 'think before you strike'. He led the miners for more than a decade and rarely got it wrong when the pithead votes were counted. The miners took his anti-strike advice in their 1981 pay dispute, Scargill's men maintained that they had been betrayed. Now, a year later, King Arthur was back to his old tricks. He called on the miners to strike, craftily linking pay with pit closures. He fulminated against the government and the Coal Board at meetings which gave him standing ovations, and he forecast a convincing victory in the strike ballot.

There were, however, strong suspicions that Scargill was using the NUM as a stalking horse for his own political pretensions. Shortly before he took over as the union's president, he wrote: 'The struggle for real control must be waged not only industrially but also politically.' He saw it as his mission to bring down Margaret Thatcher. His self-delusion was boundless, and arch-opportunist that he was, he always had an instant quote for the media he detested. But he misjudged the mood of his members. An overtime ban had already cost them dear. They could see the prospect of lost wages and dire effects on their hire purchase and mortgage commitments and on their living standards. They gave him a mortifying turndown – and this time there was no Joe Gormley to blame.

It was an earlier NUM President, Sir William Lawther, who said: 'Miners prefer practical steps in cash to the tap-dancing of the intellectuals on ideological staircases.' Scargill failed to learn that lesson in 1982. His ideological adventurism has continued to hurt the miners,

120

to wreck a once-great organization and has helped substantially to maintain the Conservatives in power – the very antithesis of his avowed objective.

Tebbit's Green Paper: union democracy

As a general election neared, unemployment was again a threat to the government's chances. Margaret Thatcher and Norman Tebbit saw another assault on the unions as their best diversionary tactic. In January 1983 Tebbit published a Green Paper on union democracy. It proposed direct ballots to counter the lack of democratic elections in many unions. It pressed home the need for pre-strike ballots. It sought to change the method for collecting the political levy, automatically paid by members of Labour-affiliated unions into Labour Party coffers unless they deliberately opted out.

The need to insist on union members giving their positive consent to political donations struck a special chord with the Alliance which deeply resented the undemocratic nature of funds shovelled over to Labour from those who might prefer to support the Tories or the Alliance. On paper, contracting out of the levy was easy. In practice, most unions made it extremely difficult to do so, and some made it well nigh impossible. Many trade unionists were unaware of their rights. What the SDP stressed, however, was the one-sidedness of Tebbit's plans to deal with union political levies while ignoring business subsidies to the Conservative Party.

Nor was Tebbit's determination to oversee trade union democracy matched by an advocacy of extended workplace democracy which might impinge on management. The SDP followed Tebbit's Green Paper with proposals on industrial democracy, recommending an enabling legal framework to allow choice and flexibility. However, the proposals had little impact.

The 1983 general election

The SDP had exploded a firecracker under the old political parties but the first flush of electoral enthusiasm, transcribed into by-election successes, was less evident now. Tory fortunes revived whereas Labour, under Foot, remained unelectable. Small wonder that Margaret Thatcher plumped for a mid-1983 general election.

I was under no illusions about Islington. It was still a Labour stronghold where the red flag flew over the town hall and Labour's dominant councillors bragged of 'Fortress Islington', their bulwark against government policies. If the town hall was a fortress, the rag, tag and bobtail defence force within made Dad's Army look like the SAS.

Even so, my only real hope was a major swing to the SDP/Liberal Alliance nationally during the campaign. That swing never materialized.

I got one highly controversial boost. My old and trusted pal Frank Chapple was the TUC's Chairman for the year. As Labour's election campaign faltered, Frank issued a personal endorsement of my SDP candidature. He had agreed to do so when it was expected that the election would be in the October, by which time his TUC chairmanship would have been over. When the June election was announced I phoned him to release him from his promise. He would have none of it. 'I want to do it,' he insisted.

He released his statement, describing me as 'a man of integrity who can be relied on to keep his promises and stand by the principles on which he fights the election'. He added: 'If you elect him, it will be a wise choice and one which you will not regret.'

It was political dynamite. An apoplectic Scargill and his NUM Communist sidekick, Mick McGahey, were quick off the mark. They branded Chapple's remarks 'outrageous' and demanded his resignation as TUC Chairman. There were plenty of other union critics. All of which ensured headline treatment for me in national and local newspapers and on TV and radio.

Scargill and company were ready to pounce at the TUC General Council. What they didn't know was that Chapple was spoiling for a scrap. He told an astonished Len Murray, prior to the meeting, that he would seek a vote of confidence and would resign if he didn't get it. At the meeting, Chapple plunged straight in with his demand for a confidence vote. David Basnett, Chairman of Trade Unions for a Labour Victory, was desperately anxious to avoid a further public confrontation which could only backfire on both the TUC and the Labour Party. He promptly moved 'next business' which was carried by nineteen votes to ten.

Scargill walked out in protest, but the row had been defused and Chapple could hardly quit in the circumstances. As he told me later, he was disappointed at the outcome. He was fed up with Labour and had a further fiery statement ready to release, had he failed to win support. In it, he pointed out that the General Council had not condemned its

Communist members who supported anti-Labour candidates and concluded: 'Ordinary decent men and women will understand that I was not prepared to compromise an honourable friendship for the sake of political expediency.' The incident showed Frank at his most typical – robust, unswerving and personally loyal.

I got another small fillip from the unions when the APEX white-collared workers' union branch at the EETPU's Bromley, Kent, headquarters, sent a £50 donation to my campaign fund, ignoring a recommendation from APEX leaders to back selected Labour candidates. Several of the branch members were old friends from my Labour Party days.

APEX, Labour-affiliated and a leading member of Trade Unions for a Labour Victory, was angered and embarrassed. It ordered the branch to cancel the cheque. I offered to return the money to avoid trouble for the local officials but those formidable ladies were not to be intimidated. They refused to back down. The affair rumbled on with a futile disciplinary inquiry long after the election was over.

The election ended my thirteen years in parliament. Defection to the SDP cost me dear. But the really bad news was that Margaret Thatcher was back in 10 Downing Street with a huge majority and that the SDP–Liberal Alliance had failed to make the breakthrough which its supporters craved for. It was not a landslide in votes, as the Tory dominance of the Commons would be based on 42.4 per cent of the overall votes cast, the fifth lowest Conservative vote since the war. Nevertheless, it gave them 397 seats and a 144-seat majority over all the other parties. The Alliance picked up a mere twenty-three seats for their 25.4 per cent of the votes. Labour took 27.6 per cent, lost 119 deposits and got 209 seats – its lowest number since 1935.

Statistically, it meant that it took 33,000 votes to elect a Conservative MP, 40,000 votes to elect a Labour MP and 340,000 votes to elect a Social Democrat or Liberal. It was a searing indictment of the British first-past-the-post electoral system and a suppression of the will of the people. Yet nothing has changed since then. Most MPs of the two major parties continue their bitter resistance to a genuinely representative democracy which might well consign many of them to the political scrap-heap.

They persist in their arguments about the need for strong and stable government, ignoring the far fairer systems operating in other European countries.

9

Of Scargillism and 'Sparks'

Extremism unfortunately begets extremism. As Thatcherism propelled the Tories sharply to the Right, the Labour movement took temporary leave of its senses as Scargillism and its unsavoury Hard Left cohorts dragooned both the TUC and the Labour Party into reckless support for a miners' strike aimed, in effect, at bringing down the elected government.

It was strange that decent, law-abiding, hardworking trade unionists could have been mesmerized by the rhetoric of Scargill and his ilk so that they elected and followed them to disaster. Perhaps more than anything, Scargillism was a reaction to Thatcherism and a belief that in Arthur Scargill the Prime Minister had met her match. That gross miscalculation was accompanied by a craven inability to declare that the union adventurer had picked the wrong fight, with the wrong weapons at the wrong time. Those in command of the Labour movement were guilty of a grave dereliction of their duty to the wider party and union membership, and to the nation.

Those leaders deserve most of the blame but it is not enough in a democracy to leave it at that. 'Trust the people' is a good slogan. Unfortunately, the people are silly enough, blind enough, idle enough, uncaring enough, selfish enough or just plain bored enough, to allow extremists to get themselves elected.

There should have been a huge public revulsion against the incursion into our national and local government of the crackpot Left and the hardline Right. The 1983 general election should have been a cakewalk for moderation. If all those who wished the SDP/Liberal Alliance well had had the courage of our convictions at the polls, the political map of Britain would have been transformed.

Instead, there was a victory for the real enemies of democracy – apathy, contempt and indifference. And for the British people's innate conservatism. 'Always keep a hold of nurse, for fear of finding something worse,' as Hilaire Belloc put it.

State of the parties: the SDP and Labour

While Scargill limbered up for his post-election onslaught, the election defeat brought inevitable changes at the top for Labour and for the SDP. Roy Jenkins was replaced by David Owen as SDP Leader after much criticism of Jenkins's performance during the election campaign. The air was thick with talk of a merger, that the Liberals and the SDP would do better as one party. It was a foretaste of troubles to come.

The Left seemed poised to tighten its grip on Labour, and this, in turn, might lead to still more desertions. For those who pulled out, as for their predecessors, the SDP offered the only route to restoring traditional Labour values of a fairer, more compassionate and more equal society. A merged party would not present the same political attraction or emotive appeal.

Neil Kinnock, poised to become Labour's leader, could hardly fail to improve on his forlorn mentor, Michael Foot. Kinnock though, remained strongly committed to the very policies so adamantly rejected by the electorate, especially unilateralism and EEC withdrawal. But his domestic party bandwagon was rolling to victory. The union block votes and the constituency parties' votes cascaded in his favour. The other candidates were also-rans. Roy Hattersley, the Right's front-runner, was never in serious contention. Peter Shore was gravely handicapped by his transparent discomfort over his party's election manifesto. Eric Heffer could not resist an ego-trip to annihilation. Kinnock reaped the benefit of Tony Benn's general election defeat and consequent ineligibility for the contest. Kinnock's left-wing credentials were dubious but, however suspect, he was the best candidate the Left had got. They thought that their support, if it failed to imprison him, would place him in their debt. It was a debt that has since been repaid by him with a hatchet job – at their expense.

The EETPU

My own problem of how to earn a living was solved when Frank Chapple asked me to help the EETPU. A few unions employed professional journalists to run their journals and their public relations, but most of them, including the EETPU, blundered along amateurishly.

Chapple had already opted to step down well ahead of normal retirement age to virtually ensure the succession for Eric Hammond, a safe pair of hands in Chapple's judgement. If it was in the union's best interests that was good enough for Chapple. Hammond had been elected as General Secretary designate. The three of us agreed that I would become the union's first-ever Head of Communications. It was an appointment that would provoke controversy because of my SDP membership. It was put to the union's Executive Council. Many of them were old friends of mine and it was unanimously endorsed.

I took up my union post early in 1984 and spent the next five and a half years at the hub of a series of overlapping conflicts and controversies which were the most volcanic in British trade union history. They culminated in the EETPU's enforced departure from the TUC, leaving what is still a seemingly unbridgeable chasm.

My formal tasks were to edit the union's newspaper *Contact* and to handle the media and public relations, promoting the union's image. I sat in on Executive Council meetings, free to speak but usually confining my contributions to my own areas of responsibility.

Chapple was a natural communicator, although his language was as garish as his neckties. He was one of life's self-educated successes. He spelled poorly, his grammar was awful, yet he read widely and rattled off ideas along with colourful and usable phrases with which I was able to spice the many articles I produced under his name. We enjoyed the kind of rapport and trust which enabled me to go ahead on his behalf with little consultation or none at all.

Chapple's virulent anti-Communism and some of the over-the-top bad advice he received made his and the union's media relations distinctly delicate. Some left-wing journalists did set out to do down the union. Others, less hostile by inclination or prejudice, became so from a reaction to EETPU misunderstanding of their attempts to play devil's advocate. I sought to achieve a more even-handed output and gradually built a situation where journalists knew that, like it or not, what they were told was reliable. They could be sure that what I said was an authoritative reflection of Chapple's viewpoint, or subsequently that of Hammond. There were friends to be helped and enemies to be resisted. But most of the time, it was possible to be non-discriminatory and to be so to the union's overall advantage.

126

TUC reaction to the NGA dispute and GCHQ union ban

Chapple had presided over the TUC's 1983 conference and confounded his critics with irrefutable home truths – 'we will have to perform the job that working people pay us to provide and stop involving ourselves in problems that we cannot solve but often only make worse.' It was a Congress that seemed at last to accept that the unions must drop their pretensions to power. The TUC's General Secretary, Len Murray, was unusually blunt. He said: 'We cannot talk as if the trade union movement is an alternative government.'

There was room at last for guarded optimism about the unions. 'New realism' was diffidently stepping out. But not for long. The old errant ways were soon resumed. First came the National Graphical Association's (NGA's) vicious dispute with Eddie Shah, proprietor of the *Stockport Messenger*. His Warrington print works was besieged. Murray courageously repudiated a TUC Employment Policy Committee pledge of support for the NGA strikers, support that was a deliberate defiance of a High Court verdict. (It was support that also ignored picket-line violence.) Clive Jenkins, leader of the white-collared ASTMS, disgracefully demanded Murray's resignation, but a TUC General Council majority eventually backed Murray and were denounced by the NGA. The episode left a fresh legacy of internal bitterness and mistrust.

The Tory government dismissed all the arguments against its ban on trade unionists at its Cheltenham intelligence headquarters, GCHQ. The government's action was vindictive, and was seen to be so by the public. The TUC snatched defeat from what might otherwise have been a public relations success. It decided on a retaliatory boycott of the National Economic Development Council, one of the few remaining forums where union leaders and ministers conversed. It was no great loss to the government, and the EETPU opposed the TUC's foolhardy decision.

The miners' strike

The year 1984 was marked by the lengthy and debilitating miners' strike. It was a masterpiece of mistiming, beginning as it did in spring, just as demand for coal was falling away. The government was ready to play for high stakes. Mrs Thatcher and her ministers knew that Arthur Scargill, a revolutionary Marxist, was intent on using the miners as shock troops to bring down the government. Defeat for Scargill would thus be the ultimate proof that union power was no more, that its teeth were drawn.

Scargill strutted and swaggered, a constant ornament to the nation's television screens. Striking miners raised funds by selling a tape of South Wales pickets singing, to the tune of the grand old hymn 'Bread of Heaven', 'Arthur Scargill, Arthur Scargill. We'll support you ever more.' Miners' wives lined up to cheer and kiss him as he visited the pit villages. They could not see that he was leading them to disaster.

At the power stations, stocks were the highest on record. The government was prepared. Mrs Thatcher, in Ian MacGregor, had her kind of man at the head of the National Coal Board. MacGregor was an elderly American tycoon with no trace about him of the conciliatory tradition that had long been the hallmark of the state-owned coal industry.

Miners' relations with other unions

Frank Chapple accurately prophesied that Scargill's proclaimed objective of job protection would be wrecked by the stoppage. He said that the overall job losses from the callous and reckless decision to shut every pit and to cripple as much of British industry as possible would continue long after the fight was over.

As the strike dragged on, a depressed and disappointed Len Murray resigned three years early from his TUC post. His eleven years in office saw a steep decline in union influence and a deeply divided movement. Already scarred by the NGA dispute, by the counter-productive TUC boycott of the NEDC and by the government's handling of the GCHQ issue, Murray was further debilitated by Scargill and the NUM. The miners' leaders deliberately bypassed the TUC as the strike hardened. Murray, a reflective and unfailingly courteous man, recovered from a heart attack, but was politically and emotionally exhausted by the constant dogfights between the government and the unions and, even more disturbing to him, that between union and union. He was not a strong leader but he worked constructively and honourably to at least keep a toehold in Whitehall's corridors of power. The government would not listen. Nor, in the end, would the bulk of the TUC General Council.

It was time too for Frank Chapple to bow out. Eric Hammond assumed the EETPU leadership mantle. Chapple, the Left's bogeyman supreme, cheerfully informed his opponents, Reagan-style, about the incoming Eric: 'You ain't seen nothing yet.' It was an accurate

128

prophecy. Hammond lacks Chapple's uncultivated flamboyance and flair. Chapple was a mixer, a jostler, who revelled in an argument with anyone, anytime, and mostly gained the advantage. Hammond is a more solitary figure, with a wry, sometimes mischievous, sense of humour. He tends to keep his own counsel, consulting few. He prepares meticulously; he calculates and nudges. Unlike the ex-Communist Chapple, Hammond has always been a Labour man. But the Communists backed him when he first stood for major office in the 'sparks' union on a left-wing ticket. It was their mistake. Both Chapple and Hammond share an overriding quality, in that they are ready to stand up and be counted. They have been the industrial counterparts of the conviction politicians of whom Thatcher and Owen are the most apparent contemporary examples. They have not been immune to the stress caused by constant vilification, but outwardly, at least, they have appeared to be fired up by it. Both are negotiators by trade and know how to cut their losses and when to back off to avert defeat.

Scargill, by contrast, was not amenable to negotiation. At the 1984 TUC conference, Hammond was one of the tiny minority prepared to go to the rostrum and insist that Scargill was grievously mistaken. But the TUC, to its shame, cobbled up a dishonest and deficient statement of total support for the miners. It was a cowardly refusal to square up to Scargill, a refusal that contributed significantly to the break-up of the once-great NUM. Hammond pointed out that the TUC failed to condemn the mounting picket-line violence, condoned the blatant abuse by the NUM of its own rules requiring a ballot before a nationwide stoppage and ignored the refusal of the miners' leaders to disavow their overt political objectives. He was barracked and jeered. 'Hitler would be proud of you lot,' he rapped back.

Hammond wrote privately to Peter Heathfield, the NUM's General Secretary, offering practical help if the miners balloted and met the other EETPU objections. It was, however, a proposal which stood little chance with the belligerent miners' leaders, and Hammond had no illusions as to its success. But it was a shrewd move in the propaganda war. It provided a valuable and justifiable retort later when the EETPU was under fire for allegedly betraying the NUM.

While other unions dithered, the EETPU's power workers were balloted. If they were to be tossed into the front line through the imposition of power blackouts, implicit in the TUC position, then the final decision must be theirs. We knew that they faced public hostility if they opted to cause widespread inconvenience and hardship.

Weeks after the TUC decision, other unions which blustered and glibly pretended that their members would back the TUC's pro-strike verdict had delivered next to nothing. Non-EETPU power station workers, workers in rail and road transport, in the docks, were in no mood for involvement in such a dubious cause. The EETPU electricity workers voted 5–1 against any action.

Support for Scargill became a touchstone for the Left. Labour's National Executive Committee, like the TUC, pledged total support and went on to attack the role of the police. Hammond denounced this as 'unworthy of a potential party of government'. Neil Kinnock duly condemned violence, but tried also to keep in step with the TUC, which belatedly endeavoured to act as peacemaker. Norman Willis, now the General Secretary, got his reward. He was humiliated by striking South Wales miners who dangled a noose in front of him at a mass rally.

Failure of the strike: its aftermath

The strike crumbled, but Scargill remained intransigent. He brazened out revelations about a Libyan connection and court action by working miners about his control of strike funds. The drift back to work was under way. In a speech to a conference organized by the CBI, I said: 'Miners' leaders talk self-righteously about the dishonour of trade unionists who refuse to support them. What greater dishonour is there than to wilfully and knowingly lead ordinary decent people to defeat and then to refuse to accept the responsibility for that situation?'

It was March 1985 when Scargill's bruised and broken army accepted their failure, but their braggadocio general made no such admission. 'You have won the greatest battle of all by struggling against the government's policies,' he told his members. It was the gibbering of a fallen idol, who had boasted that he would not give an inch, that he would compel the enemy's unconditional surrender.

What of Scargill's achievements? The exhausted miners lost a year's wages, and some were in debt for years to come; some never worked again. No pits were saved. Miners' families were divided. The NUM itself was bankrupted and irrevocably fractured as the breakaway Union of Democratic Mineworkers was no passing blip on the union screen. The cost to the nation, to all of us, was enormous.

Most importantly, Scargill had openly challenged the government of the day and lost. Mass picketing was defeated and the police protected the right to work of those who wished to do so, despite intimidation, provocation and violence.

The sacrifices of striking miners and their families produced much public respect, even admiration, for the underdogs. The Coal Board's MacGregor promoted sympathy for the miners with public obduracy that sometimes matched Scargill's. Nor was Mrs Thatcher the clear beneficiary of Scargillism as she might have assumed would be her due. There were opinion poll indications that the public now wanted a period of peace and that Thatcherism was not the readily perceived means to secure this end.

Yet one lesson was paramount, one near-certain prediction was possible. No trade union, no combination of unions, would for the foreseeable future dare to throw down the political gauntlet, to seek to overthrow the rule of law by deliberately confronting a government, to pit workers against the state, to use industrial might for blatant political ends.

Neither Scargill nor anyone else in the union's leadership accepted responsibility for the catastrophe which engulfed the NUM. Instead, Scargill sought scapegoats: the TUC, the Labour leaders, the UDM and 'scab' working miners, and, of course, other 'scab' unions and particularly the electricians. We were all to blame, and still are, as each pit closure is used to say, in effect, 'don't blame me – I told you so'. At Labour's 1985 conference, Eric Hammond was jeered and abused once more, this time for opposing the NUM's demand that a future Labour government should reimburse fines imposed during the strike. Hammond called the miners 'lions led by donkeys'. But the NUM motion was carried – against Neil Kinnock's wishes.

Slowly though, the myth of Scargill's prowess has faded. The grim aftermath of the stoppage for so many of those involved, the confusing story of the strike funds, the remorseless and continuing rundown of membership, the ridiculous refusal to negotiate alongside the despised UDM, have turned Scargill into an industrial has-been and a political never-was.

The miners' strike provided another seemingly obvious, but often disregarded, home truth: that a union that can explain its case lucidly will achieve far better media treatment than one that cannot. The NUM's public relations flopped. Scargill, playing to his militant gallery, regularly lambasted the media and gained massive personal exposure. But his self-centred projection was no match for the communications strategy and expensive public relations machinery of

131

the Coal Board and the government. It is useless for unions to eschew professional help, ignoring the need for planned public relations and then blaming the media when things go wrong. A communications strategy is vital and every union should have one.

The EETPU: the new model union

The EETPU acquired a public relations shine, but only by comparison with the slow-moving, secretive bureaucracies that most unions remain. Ideas get pigeonholed by union functionaries or officials with horizons that are limited to their union office or past shopfloor experience. Few union officials understand the need to initiate rather than react, to be prepared to exploit the media to their organization's advantage. It is not only left-wingers who treat the media with hostility and then complain with anguish that they are misunderstood. The EETPU displayed similar faults, and still does, though I like to think that I made some progress.

That said, the EETPU was different. 'Different and proud of it' was the message I concocted for Chapple and Hammond jointly in a glossy colour brochure, which I produced to break new ground by marketing the union directly to employers. All the benefits of our pragmatic approach were set out in the kind of language which even the dullest managing director would find intelligible. Employers were freely quoted, telling the world of our merits. So were ministers. Norman Tebbit praised our 'progressive approach'. Later we printed a picture and quotation from Tom King, who replaced Tebbit as Employment Secretary, in the updated brochure. We aimed especially to persuade employers in the high-tech 'sunrise' industries to sign single union deals with us, sending out an initial 500 copies to targeted firms. 'The EETPU', we told them, is 'the Union for today and tomorrow'. Many of the new high-tech firms were Japanese, and to woo them we sent a two-man mission to Japan, briefcases full of brochures translated into Japanese.

The *Daily Telegraph* reported that the brochure astonished British managers. It said: 'It is as far from the world of Arthur Scargill and short-sighted union propaganda as it is possible to get.' The EETPU was setting a trend and was 'far ahead of the field' in the fightback by unions against membership losses.

But union criticism of our pioneering single-union strike-free agreements built up. There were several attempts to force us to withdraw from them. The drive against us was keenest in South Wales where Japanese inwards-investment was substantial and the TGWU resented our impact.

Our single-union deals differed from company to company, but the main ingredients were: single status for blue- and white-collar workers, with parity of working hours, holidays and other benefits; training and retraining, linked to job flexibility; and elected consultative bodies with access to the kind of information more usually kept secret in British industry. The strike-free element was usually binding pendulum arbitration. If normal negotiations broke down, an independent arbitrator decided in favour of either the company offer or the union claim. The difference could not be split. So both sides aimed at consensus rather than risk outright rejection by the arbitrator. We stressed that all these deals were based on workforce and management consent and could be ended by either side giving due notice.

Much of this was unoriginal. Binding arbitration operated at the former Upper Clyde Shipbuilders. There were several industry-wide agreements of this kind, including our own in electrical contracting. The Civil Service unions put a 'no disruption' option to the government during the GCHQ row. Mirror Group print unions were ready to make the same kind of bargain to prevent Robert Maxwell's company takeover.

Hypocrisy was rife. The TUC General Council proposed that unions which made such agreements must first get the consent of other interested unions. The decision was aimed unerringly at us and would give our rivals a blanket veto in a key area of our industrial activity. It was all building up towards an unavoidable showdown. Behind it was the burgeoning recruitment war between unions, snarling and scrapping over a shrinking membership carcase. Whatever we did was seen by our rivals as part of that wider struggle.

The ballot issue

The EETPU's centralized, comprehensive, computerized membership records – a longstanding Chapple innovation – were commended by ministers as vital to trade union democracy and damned by the Left as paving the way to statutory balloting requirements.

There was a furore over the union's decision to apply for public funds for postal ballots, thus flouting TUC boycott policy. Norman Willis brought the TUC Employment Committee to our Executive Council meeting to ask us to change our minds. The TUC took 'tainted' government money to run its education services without a twinge of conscience. Why not cash for ballots? There was certainly no principle at stake. Willis and Co. got a unanimous turndown. Eric Hammond astutely played it long with our application for a £200,000 hand-out. The engineering union plunged straight in, received £1,200,000 from the government and took the brunt of the TUC wrath. The engineers balloted their members who voted 10–1 to take the money. We were the good guys, standing firmly by our AUEW allies, but not yet in the dock ourselves. There was much speculation that the AUEW, the TUC's second biggest affiliate, would link with us to form a rival power centre to the TUC. We balloted our members and got similarly overwhelming approval for the ballot fund cash.

TUC leaders looked over the precipice and, for once, had the sense to draw back. They fudged the issue at the 1985 Congress, where EETPU speakers were hissed at before they ever reached the rostrum. The TUC capitulation was just as well for everyone. We said that we would walk out if the AUEW was disciplined. Our local electricians were ready to black-out the conference in protest. The engineers were allowed time to ballot their members again. They did so and got the same result. With the conference behind it, the TUC General Council changed course dramatically – by thirty-nine votes to six. Norman Willis said that he was not in the market 'for putting a finger in the dam'. (But for this belated U-turn, the TUC would have had to expel about a seventh of its decreasing membership. More and more unions were applying for state funds. Now, there are few that do not do so. It was a massive non-issue, fanned by left-wing zealotry into a crisis that could have wrecked the TUC.)

The ballot money rumpus was another sign of the storms to come over individual union sovereignty. Eric Hammond insisted that our members elected our Executive Council to be responsible for the finance and government of the union, none of which was the TUC's business.

Other issues: market unionism, acceptance of the UDM

I set up several further initiatives which infuriated the Left. We held our own EETPU fringe meeting at the Confederation of British Industry's annual conference. Eric was the main speaker and I chaired a packed gathering. There was plenty of media coverage for what was a unique occasion. There was an erroneous report that we intended to apply for

134

CBI membership, which, though unfounded, helped us to keep a high profile.

Even more controversially, we invited Norman Tebbit, the Tory most loathed by the unions, to open our new robotics and inter-active video-disc-training facility at our training college at Cudham, Kent. Tebbit was now Industry Secretary. His department had chipped in with a £95,000 grant towards the cost of the £150,000 project, so he was the correct minister to ask. But the Left was infuriated and no one from any other union dared to turn up.

Another of our 'crimes' was to indulge in 'market unionism'. I organized a well-publicized press conference at London's Waldorf Hotel where we launched an unprecedented package of financial benefits and services for our 350,000 members. That size of membership allowed us to negotiate advantageous rates on services, from unit trusts, for car breakdown and recovery, life, house and car insurance, accident benefit, savings and pension schemes, share advice and a variety of extras. Some other unions did some of this, but the totality of our package was novel. If we did it, our rivals had to denounce it. Hypocrisy gleamed brightly as most other unions, notably the General, Municipal and Boilermakers, straggled behind us with similar arrangements. The are all 'market unionists' now.

The EETPU was becoming increasingly isolated within the TUC but not from our own members. Yet what we did today, the rest did tomorrow. The EETPU's industrial training colleges and programmes are a jewel in the union's crown and have earned worldwide commendation. Courses are marketed to employers. Unemployed members are trained and retrained at the union's expense. Once again, other unions have copied the EETPU prototype.

Our pro-NATO, anti-unilateralist speakers were regularly shut out of TUC and Labour Party defence debates, for theirs was an unpopular message, sure to raise the temperature among delegates. Nowadays, however, the EETPU position is contemporary wisdom.

The EETPU compiled a list of a hundred single-union deals involving most major unions. Some of those deals were made at the expense of electricians' jobs where other unions refused to recognize our members' union cards and squeezed them out. So much for brotherhood. Now deals of this kind, with a strike-free element included, have spread. Other unions, however, dress them up to avoid formal TUC disapproval.

There was more trouble when the union proffered the hand of

friendship to the Union of Democratic Mineworkers. UDM and EETPU representatives attended a joint energy policy conference. There was talk of a merger. The EETPU faced more TUC enmity and received another slap on the wrist.

Today and the EETPU

Trouble was so easy to come by, courted or by accident. We were back in the firing line over a potential single-union agreement with Eddie Shah, who had moved on from his dispute with the NGA to seek to fulfil his ambition to publish a national newspaper on a greenfield site. He foresaw a venture that would not be in hock to the plethora of restrictive practices imposed on Fleet Street by the print unions. The EETPU had a sizeable printing industry membership. Both Chapple and Hammond held the view that modern technology should allow journalists and electricians only to produce newspapers. Shah's harsh experience with the NGA meant that he wanted his proposed national newspaper, *Today*, to be non-union.

It seemed to me that we should have a crack at persuading Shah that he could do business with us. Lord Harris, the former Labour Party Press Officer and by now an SDP peer, was on Shah's board of directors. I telephoned him and a meeting was arranged. Eric Hammond, Tom Rice, who headed our white-collar section and also handled the printing industry, and I breakfasted with Shah and Harris at the London hotel, which was Shah's temporary headquarters. The meeting went well. We talked a bit of politics. Shah admired Thatcher but was no convinced Tory. He insisted that he was not hostile to unions but the print unions were something apart. It appeared to be fertile ground.

My introductory job was done, and a draft agreement was discussed, but nothing was settled. Meanwhile, the print union, SOGAT, tried to sabotage Shah's plans. Senior SOGAT officials sought to pressurize the National Bank of Hungary, through the Hungarian ambassador and that country's unions, to withdraw a £7 million commercial loan to 'strike-breaker' Shah. One unnamed SOGAT official talked chillingly of 'blood on the streets' if Asian shopkeepers handled the new daily in London.

However, SOGAT's attitude changed. It met EETPU officials to see if it could find a legitimate role for its members on Shah's paper. It could see that his plan to produce *Today* with a satellite system from five or six provincial centres could leave it out in the cold, alongside the NGA. SOGAT pragmatism prevailed.

But ownership of *Today* switched to Lonrho, the multinational company which owned the *Observer*, and which recognized the traditional print unions. It was cool towards any deal with the EETPU at *Today*. In turn, News International took over. That was more promising for the EETPU, but nothing has since transpired.

This unsatisfactory episode was, though, the precursor of an historic and bloody dispute involving the EETPU, the other print unions and News International, Rupert Murdoch's print empire. It was a dispute which was to revolutionize the national newspaper industry in Britain and to spell the end for Fleet Street.

10

Warpath to Wapping

Whether the newspaper tycoon Rupert Murdoch would have achieved his rout of the print unions and his overall Wapping success story without EETPU assistance is arguable. But his relentless determination, tenacity and single-mindedness indicate that he would have done so. It would though, have been a far more problematical journey for him.

Wapping demonology lives on, and there are print union leaders who still regard me as the villain of the piece, the instigator of the EETPU's involvement in the conflict. They are mistaken in this, but in May 1985 I inadvertently brought together two of the principal players in the ensuing events. I arranged a lunch for Eric Hammond with the *News of the World*'s then Editor, David Montgomery, and several senior editorial staff. Eric and I arrived at the newspaper's dining room, just off Fleet Street, to find an additional and apparently self-invited luncheon guest: Bruce Matthews, News International's Managing Director and Murdoch's right-hand man. Matthews subsequently asked Hammond to join him for a one-to-one private chat. It seems that it was then that the possibility of sole recognition for the EETPU at Wapping was first mooted, certainly that the seeds of continuing contact were sown.

The difficulties of a smooth transition from Fleet Street were symbolized for well over two years by the silent plant at the company's Wapping site, just along the Thames from Tower Bridge. It threatened to become a £72 million white elephant. But Murdoch knew that the print unions, fragmented and warring among themselves, could not withstand progress indefinitely, that new technology was inevitable and that demanning was bound to follow. The unrestrained union grip was loosening. SOGAT talked openly of its own single-union deal with News International to overcome NGA obstruction to the move to Wapping, intended initially for the *Sun* and the *News of the World*.

Murdoch had had his bellyful of commercial desecration from both SOGAT and the NGA. Ideally, he would have preferred no unions at his plant, but the EETPU was the least unattractive option and could have its uses. He was hell-bent on sweeping advances, above all an end to the print unions' age-old stranglehold on the newspaper industry through their veto on management's right to hire and fire.

State of Fleet Street

Britain's national press has been damned again and again by independent investigations into its industrial relations practices and their appalling consequences for the industry's economic health. The last major probe, the McGregor Royal Commission, reported in 1977 that there was 'no alternative to root-and-branch change in Fleet Street'. It warned starkly of the 'reckless disregard of peril' shown by the chapels, the union workplace organizations, and by the workers, all apparent in a 'suicidal' spate of unofficial stoppages.

Far from improving, post-McGregor, the industrial relations climate became still more poisonous. Overmanning, absenteeism and inter-union acrimony remained entrenched. More pay for less work was the effective slogan, and industrial blackmail was a built-in daily occurrence.

The McGregor criticisms broke no new ground. They were pre-empted by a Royal Commission in 1962, by an Economist Intelligence Unit exposure in 1967 and by condemnatory Prices and Incomes Board reports in 1967 and 1970. All spoke harshly about the labour relations jungle and the need for drastic change.

Yet newspapers, often in the red, abysmally managed and ludicrously overstaffed, kept going. Their lifeline tended to be cross-subsidization from owners' non-newspaper interests, coupled with a curious non-commercial proprietorial mixture of paternalism, power-lust and the genuine excitement of running a newspaper. Employees were convinced that it was a lifeline that would always keep them afloat. That philosophy was at the heart of much of the malpractice. Someone, the workforce reckoned, would always pick up the tab, whatever their Luddite excesses.

The best chance for reform came from recommendations in an

interim report in 1976 from the McGregor Commission and in an associated study by ACAS (the Advisory, Conciliation and Arbitration Service). The union leaders and the newspaper publishers reacted favourably and put forward far-reaching proposals in a Programme for Action. The all-powerful chapels refused to believe that the industry faced a crisis. They voted the package down. Fleet Street's big breakthrough to reality was stillborn.

The Thatcher government's subsequent restrictive laws on secondary action inhibited the militants. But overmanning remained rife in the eighties. More and more operatives went missing, on pay, while managements turned a blind eye. 'Spanish' practices, the ingenious variety of restrictions used to gain extra cash for no extra effort, were as prevalent as ever. So was the ritual exploitation of the perishability of the product – the 'pay up or no paper' shotgun tactic.

Management continued to surrender to buy peace. They saw what happened when the Thomson Organization, then owners of Times Newspapers, took a stand in 1978–9. An eleven-month suspension of the group's publications found the unions proclaiming eventual victory and, judged by the industry's twisted logic, entitled to do so. Lord Thomson put *The Times* and the *Sunday Times* up for sale. He gave his reasons succinctly: 'The unions have been impossible to live with. We haven't been able to implement the things we wanted to do to save these papers. We have tried and failed.' Undertakings given by the unions were not honoured. They refused to co-operate with new technology.

Rupert Murdoch's £12 million bid rescued the newspapers from closure. Murdoch drove a hard bargain, particularly over manning levels. However, the same old troubles soon broke out and Murdoch threatened to shut his newly acquired papers.

The early eighties saw ugly disputes at the *Observer*, the *Financial Times* and the *Daily Telegraph*. Unions scrapped with each other, but employer disunity was just as marked. An agreement among pro-prietors to compensate each other when one paper was hit was abandoned.

Print union malpractice

Fleet Street was the scene of an unending guerrilla war between managements and chapels, sapping morale and wrecking efficiency. Not all the full-time union officials were guilty of drinking on empty heads. There were those who privately acknowledged that what went on

140

in the name of trade unionism had no relevance to the honourable concepts of brotherhood and solidarity. Industrial relations in the national press were a racket, bordering on the criminal. Each man was his own entrepreneur and saw himself as dealing in like terms with unscrupulous bosses.

Basic pay rates were supplemented by incredible levies, sometimes for work which was never done. Operators 'hammered the docket' – filled in their own pay sheets. Mostly, they were unchecked. Each day brought some fresh skirmish aimed at producing an extra payment. If management wanted an edition to catch a train, they might find that a chapel had called a meeting in the middle of a print-run, a printing press would mysteriously go wrong, a reel of paper might break or a stacker would jam.

Sunday newspapermen referred sarcastically to 'hawk Monday, dove Saturday'. (Sunday papers tended to be the big earners, and management resolve to withstand chapel demands weakened as the weekend deadline neared.) The Sunday papers stood to lose far more from a shut-down than did most of their daily brethren, as they were more vulnerable. The 'Saturday night stick-up' was another phrase which accurately described the situation.

Earnings throughout Fleet Street were excessive by comparison with the rest of British industry, but the biggest scandal was the money handed over, with management and chapel connivance, to those who were not needed and did not attend.

Many well-paid print workers had plenty of time and money to invest in running their own enterprises on the side. 'Working the bingo' was common. The four-week shift was the norm, but the men only turned up for two shifts, sometimes only one, while their mates covered for them. One overseer on a Spanish holiday met a publishing department employee from his newspaper and was told unashamedly: 'I'm on a fortnight's bingo.' Print-workers owned taxis, mini-cabs, pubs, restaurants and shops. One chapel official, with a pilot's licence, ferried VIPs in his private plane to race meetings and hired out his two Rolls Royce motor cars for functions. Another chapel official regularly invited newspaper executives to shoots on his farm. Fleet Street had more than its share of first-class golfers. Printers lived as far away as Cornwall and Wales, and one reputedly commuted from France.

A 40 per cent attendance to run the presses was regarded as high. Holidays could account for twelve weeks of a year. One Sunday newspaper paid staff to work each Saturday – but gave them one Saturday off in every two . 'Ghost' workers, with phoney pay-packets that were shared out, lingered on, despite Inland Revenue efforts to stamp out the practice. What made all this possible was the tight chapel control of labour supply through the closed shop. Chapel officials were known to take kickbacks for placing men in work. Management was unlikely to know the names of those due to work a particular shift, as the chapel took care of such matters.

There were countless demarcation disputes, often over the proposed introduction of new technology. Expensive new equipment lay unused for years because of union refusal to agree manning levels.

Lurid anecdotes are legion, but these assertions are not based on hearsay. Those involved would not talk on the record, but extensive disclosures in earlier probes, together with my own checks and cross-checks, leave me in no doubt as to their veracity. Fleet Street was a mixture of black comedy, ineptitude, cowardice and villainy. And it simply couldn't last. Conservative legislation produced an increased readiness by proprietors to go to law. The NGA fracas with Eddie Shah at Warrington cost the union £675,000 in fines, with a further £125,000 in damages. It was an expensive lesson for the NGA, and national newspapers were soon to follow Shah's example, with several of them obtaining High Court injunctions to thwart union militancy.

By the mid-eighties, most major newspaper groups planned to move their main printing operations from Fleet Street to London's dock-lands. The NGA, in particular, had scant claim to operate the electronic, computer-based technology which would run the newspaper of the future. Direct input computer technology scrapped the traditional composing room and with it the need for NGA presence. The NGA's defence was to demand that its displaced members should 'follow the job' into other departments. But that was no permanent solution, simply a desperate rearguard action.

Fleet Street, protected from the harsh winds of foreign competition, showed signs of reluctantly doing what provincial newspapers and the newspaper industries of America, Japan and other advanced indus-trialized nations did long before. In 1985 Eddie Shah stormed Fleet Street with *Today*, and Robert Maxwell, a powerful and unsettling influence who was out to slash manning levels, strutted the *Mirror* stage. United Newspapers now owned the Express Group and demanded redundancies. Most significantly, Rupert Murdoch skilfully prepared for the right moment to press the detonator that was to cause the biggest explosion of all (one which would catapult the EETPU, again, to the brink of departure from the TUC).

Murdoch triumphant: the move to Wapping

The print unions lacked the nous and comprehension to thwart Murdoch. There was trouble over recognition at his proposed new London evening paper, the *Post*. The EETPU sought a single-union deal. The other print unions resisted plans to shift existing titles to Wapping, and demanded a 'jobs for life' agreement for all their members – an open-ended promise that they had no prospect of gaining. News International gave them six months' notice that their agreements would be terminated. That, the NGA and SOGAT claimed later, amounted to deliberate provocation. Their response was an industrial action ballot and a strike which closed the company's Fleet Street operations (or, more accurately, plant at nearby Bouverie Street and Grays Inn Road). The 5,500 workers were immediately deemed by News International to have dismissed themselves.

If Murdoch was out for a showdown – and there seems little doubt that he was – the print unions played right into his hands. They allowed themselves to be manœuvred into a no-win situation. The possibility of a Murdoch flit to Wapping was widely peddled in advance, but the print unions could not bring themselves to believe that he would really risk it. Theirs was a mixture of arrogant self-confidence, defiance and sheer stupidity. Even now, they still seek to vilify others, to produce scapegoats to account for their self-imposed demise.

Murdoch's was an audacious masterpiece of planning, kept under the closest wraps to the last. Security was as tight as Crossmaglen's. Only a handful of key executives on each newspaper was forewarned. Virtually overnight, Murdoch switched around 35 per cent of Fleet Street's output to its new docklands home. It was a staggering coup.

The EETPU had refused to take part in a fruitless common negotiating approach to News International with the other print unions. Eric Hammond was scathing about a SOGAT publication which contained 'a thinly veiled call to violence – to fit me up with a couple of concrete boots'. More to the point, the EETPU leadership saw a real prospect of assuming the major role in the 'electronic unionism' which would be justified by the print industry's new technology. Its members, it believed, were more relevant to the newspapers of the future than those with outdated skills, or no skills, who clung to their jobs courtesy of a protective print union mafia. The NGA could seek to 'follow the job', but the EETPU was out to 'follow the electron', all the way to Wapping. Moreover, the print unions were led by left-wingers, and

Communist influence was strong. There was no political love lost between the EETPU and its Fleet Street union rivals.

Trouble at Wapping

Murdoch had a further trump to play: the law. The government had changed the rules of the industrial relations' game. Murdoch created a separate company for his Wapping plant, which made all action taken against him by the sacked print workers secondary and thus illegal. The TUC ordered sanctions against the company and ran into News International writs. Mass picketing was not prevented, but a High Court order led to SOGAT's £17 million assets being seized and a £25,000 fine was imposed.

There were violent scenes as the police held back demonstrators – up to 7,000 of them at the peak of the battle. Newspaper lorries had windscreens smashed, drivers were assaulted and there were arson attacks on outlying warehouses. 'Fortress Wapping' was protected by high fences and razor wire. Ministers were forcefully condemnatory of the thuggery. Labour confined its support for the sacked printers to little more than a refusal to talk to News International journalists, a boycott only partially observed by Labour MPs, and one which caused the participants more frustration than the targeted newspapers. The unions failed to stop either production or distribution of the newspapers which went on to record sales.

If Murdoch's move to Wapping was a D-day secret, then so too was the EETPU's early entanglement. The key figure in the operation was Tom Rice, Dublin-born national official for the printing industry. (I first met Tom in 1960 when he was still in the Communist Party, but disgruntled and at the point of departure. He is likeable, but a natural cloak-and-dagger man. He enjoys a plot and would readily admit to it.)

The EETPU and bussing

Communication, not conspiracy, was my job. I was torn between the need to know and a feeling that it might be better not to. What I didn't know I couldn't pass on to inquisitive journalists. Ignorance though, undermined the credibility I had painstakingly built up on the union's behalf and was not my style. It made life difficult. Eric Hammond too, played his cards close to the chest. I winkled out a sketchy account of what was happening but it was media enquiries which first alerted me to

144

strange goings on in Southampton where, it seemed, our officials co-operated in recruiting members to be bussed daily through the hostile picket lines and into the Wapping plant.

BBC Radio's Labour Correspondent, Nicholas Jones, writing in the *Listener*, said that the EETPU 'has been buoyed up by adroit publicity'. The electricians, he explained, were first off the mark in the race to communicate with the news media, thus capturing the headlines and leaving the TUC trailing in our wake. We knew, he said, that we could shape the news if we could help reporters meet their deadlines. He said:'Eric Hammond, the EETPU's General Secretary, and the union's Head of Communications, John Grant, make a formidable team. Once again, the TUC has been caught off guard: Norman Willis and his colleagues at Congress House have failed to take account of the fact that the eighth largest affiliate has shown the sharpest news sense among the 90 trade unions in the TUC.'

But Jones, an astute and conscientious reporter, was far too kind. We never had a communications strategy, much as I would have welcomed it. I flew daily by the seat of my pants, sometimes well-informed, often scrabbling for crumbs of information from colleagues who were short of time, reluctant to give anything away and unable to accept my necessary deadline priorities. That 'aggressive' staff comprised one young lady assistant, wearing journalistic L-plates, and a secretary. We had no fax machine, no direct news service hook-up, unlike many other unions. Ours was an unsatisfactory makeshift operation. Still, despite the handicaps, it worked tolerably well. Our opponents had too many shortcomings and problems of their own to notice ours.

The story that the EETPU put out on bussing was that the union had helped recruitment for Wapping via an agency, merely on a short-term basis, to prepare the plant. The workers concerned were then offered the chance to stay on, and they took it. It was a possible, even plausible, explanation, but not easy to sell to rightly sceptical journalists. The EETPU's recruitment aid to Murdoch was always the weakest aspect of the union's defence against its critics. Those critics included print unions which used the closed shop unscrupulously to recruit their own chosen brethren, mafia-style. It was noticeable, for instance, that blacks and women were absent from Fleet Street composing rooms. The other unions were heavy with cant.

Whatever the so-called moral case against us on recruitment, there were sound practical reasons which indicated that we should never have got into the business. Not to have done so might well have debarred us from the sole recognition at Wapping which was the anticipated reward. Yet the numbers concerned, a few hundred at best, were never likely to be worth the dangerous game. Nor has that reward been achieved. The smoke and gunfire have cleared, the EETPU is no longer inhibited by TUC membership, but it still has no worthwhile recognition at Wapping.

Other union involvement at Wapping

If the EETPU made mistakes, it could take some consolation from the hypocrisy and double standards of its union critics. SOGAT and the NGA scrapped viciously over the years, while the NGA's Tony Dubbins had the effrontery to urge the EETPU to 'act like a decent brotherly trade union'. TNT, the transport firm responsible for Wapping newspaper distribution, was a TGWU closed shop. There was no serious attempt by that union to discipline its drivers for trundling their lorries nightly past the barricades and the enraged pickets. SOGAT failed to win the support of its own members outside London when it tried to stop distribution. There was little SOGAT sympathy for the Fleet Street élite elsewhere in the union – or in other unions. Many journalists went to work, and the NUJ fumed to minimal effect. In total, some thousands of print union, NUJ and TGWU members worked to produce and distribute News International's various publications, whereas the EETPU never had more than a couple of hundred members at Wapping.

TUC v. EETPU

The print unions turned to the TUC to act against the EETPU, and the TUC General Council duly arraigned us on seven charges for actions which other unions claimed 'imperilled' the jobs of the sacked printers. The basis of the case was the EETPU's role in recruitment of Wapping's special workforce.

The EETPU planned its defence at its Hayes Court headquarters. Eric Hammond, jostled and kicked by pickets at TUC headquarters, delivered a detailed response. It was, he asserted, the print unions' premature strike action which imperilled their members' job. It was not EETPU behaviour that was detrimental. 'Any objective review of industrial relations . . . would indict a number of trade unions who would make better candidates for such a charge.' The case against the

146

EETPU, he declared, was motivated by political prejudice and membership ambitions. Our lawyers had been busy – prodded along by Eric. He had digested the lessons of his moderate predecessors who had used the law so effectively to free the union from its one-time Communist shackles. Now he warned the TUC that if it required the EETPU to instruct its members at Wapping to stop work it would be tantamount to asking them to break their employment contracts. The EETPU would be conspiring in secondary action, outside the law; it would see the TUC in court first.

The TUC got its own legal advice, but we were right. Ron Todd, Ken Gill and others on the General Council Left were spoiling for an eyeball-to-eyeball scrap. They calculated that our suspension and subsequent expulsion from the TUC for defying its edicts would make it open season for them to poach our membership. Despite the lawyers' views, it was a narrow squeak. The General Council held back from directing us to order our Wapping members to walk out – by fifteen votes to fourteen. We were found guilty on five of the seven charges. Half-a-dozen TUC directives were issued to stop us helping any further recruitment, to prevent unilateral negotiations with News International and to prevent us from signing any sole negotiating agreement which excluded other unions from recognition.

Our Executive Council had a simple choice: accept the directives or face ultimate expulsion from the TUC. I was convinced that the TUC had erected another insuperable obstacle to our continuing right to make single-union deals of our choice. But this was not the time to fight it out. There was no public sympathy for the print unions, but we were less than lilywhite. The Executive Council accepted the directives, and further action against the EETPU was prevented. The print unions were left impotent and complaining, like the Communist *Morning Star*, at the TUC's 'weak-kneed' stance.

The acceptance of the directives relieved the enormous pressure on Eric Hammond. The strain on him from the sustained hate campaign was considerable and it showed. (He and his wife, Brenda, had been subjected to unpleasant and threatening phone calls at their home.) The rest of us too had been under some strain, as there were printers' pickets at the union offices, and we were all concerned with personal safety. We realized, however, that the threat was less from the understandably embittered print workers than from the various extremists who had infiltrated their picket lines.

Once the EETPU had accepted the TUC directives, Hammond,

hitherto the *enfant terrible*, became the peace envoy, the TUC's go-between with Murdoch. One thing was certain: that Murdoch would not retreat from his pledge never to have the traditional print unions at Wapping or at its sister plant in Glasgow. The strike dragged on, and Murdoch made several attempts to settle it with compensation payments. The unions, however, consistently rejected his offers. The sacked printers were invited by the company to apply individually for compensation, and thus the stubborn ranks were pierced. The end was in sight, and a steady stream of applications for compensation flowed. The pickets dwindled.

A mass rally to mark the first anniversary of the strike ended in the worst-ever riot outside Wapping. More than 200 people, mainly policemen, were injured in what was a last despairing gesture. Within days, first SOGAT then the NGA called off the conflict. The NUJ was the last to back down. It had been altogether a futile thirteen months.

SOGAT's London activists cried treachery. Their relationship with their General Secretary, Brenda Dean, had always been uneasy. They rejected her earlier recommendations to accept severance pay, and smarted over the commitment she won at the union's delegate conference: that SOGAT's funds should never again be put in danger of sequestration. They ignored the fact that half of the union's £17 million assets were spent on the dispute.

SOGAT leaders publicly condemned the EETPU, but they privately despaired at the behaviour of their own hardcore strikers, some of them ringleaders in the ugly scenes outside Wapping. (So much so that they leaked details of one picket-line thug with a previous prison sentence for beating up a policeman. The *Sun* was poised to run the story, only to find that it was a spent conviction, handed out too long ago to allow details to be printed without breaking the law.)

The ferocity of the battles between police and pickets was a major factor in the unions' defeat. The grim tally was nearly 1,500 arrests and more than 550 police officers, and scores of demonstrators, injured. The public was never behind workers who they regarded as overpaid and underworked. It was the harassed and besieged police, seen nightly on the TV news bulletins, who had that vital public support without which no industrial action is likely to succeed. People rightly resented the enormous cost to public funds of policing the dispute. It was the unions, not Murdoch or the government, who shouldered the blame.

The capitulation of the once-invincible print unions was another triumph for Thatcherism, as the government's anti-union legislation hamstrung the unions throughout the strike. News International hammered home a final blow after the riotous anniversary rally, securing the reactivation of a court order which banned all further mass picketing.

Ostensibly, the EETPU was now the TUC's most promising route towards a permanent solution to the Wapping dispute. The friction between us and the TUC was much reduced. Trust, however, had yet to be regained – and never was.

There was enough movement by the TUC for the EETPU to justify its decision to go along with the Wapping directives. The shift by the TUC over ballot monies and the increased isolation of Arthur Scargill were indications that things were moving our way. Still to be faced was the virtual veto on strike-free deals, but a temporary *rapprochement* was in order.

A recognition agreement at News International would have benefited the EETPU, since it already had the only sizeable group of non-journalistic trade unionists inside the Wapping plant. No deal meant a non-union operation. Hammond went through the motions of persuading Murdoch's men to reopen talks with the print unions. He flew to the United States for an unproductive meeting with Murdoch, who, having fought and won, was unlikely to give away his advantage. The talks were not helped by the NGA, which threatened to renew its calls for the EETPU's expulsion from the TUC unless a settlement was achieved which secured recognition, some jobs and further compensation for sacked printers.

The union ran into more flak on the eve of the 1986 TUC conference. There were allegations in a book, *The End of the Street*, by Linda Melvern, which suggested EETPU collusion at national level with News International over Wapping. There were claims that the union had not come clean in its earlier arguments with the TUC General Council. The NGA's Tony Dubbins seized on a Congress decision to reject the General Council's previous verdict that the EETPU should not be directed to instruct its members to stop working at Wapping. He tried to force the issue back onto the TUC agenda.

The EETPU met at Hayes Court to consider its reply. Eric Hammond floated the possibility that we might tell SOGAT that we would ballot our Wapping members to ask them if they would transfer. I said that this ran contrary to all that we had said about our right to represent people in the industry. Those members would not go away, anyway, as they had been intimidated and threatened. It would be seen as a pointless ploy. Tom Rice didn't like the idea either and it was dropped.

Hammond was understandably tired of the newspaper industry. Relations with News International had deteriorated. Our own Fleet Street electricians were under left-wing leadership and historically troublesome. It was hardly surprising that Hammond was guarded when the *Mirror*'s ebullient Robert Maxwell made an undercover approach to him about a future single-union deal.

The NGA worried away at us. Norman Willis argued at the TUC General Council that the EETPU had already been tried by the TUC and found guilty on charges that included recruiting for Wapping. It was against natural justice, he said, for the union to be tried twice for the same offence. 'That's true whether you are running a club or the Old Bailey,' he declared. Eric Hammond flatly denied that he or any other EETPU official gave the go-ahead for the company to print at Wapping, one of the new allegations against us. The General Council backed Willis, but by an unconvincing twenty-three votes to twenty-one.

Hammond admitted to journalists that the EETPU's standing with other unions was weakened by Wapping. But not its standing with ordinary trade unionists or with our own members. He said: 'When I am going round the country talking to our members and Wapping comes up, they say: "Good on you. Give 'em some more." ' That was certainly so. Within the union's Executive Council, however, there were growing misgivings. Until now there had been total unity, and a gung-ho spirit. However, as we headed for the 1987 TUC Conference there were fresh claims that Tom Rice had breached the TUC directives. The *Guardian* got hold of a document which suggested that he had been 'in constant contact' with Wapping management. The document indicated various joint activities.

A new row with the TUC and print unions was certain. To try and head it off, the union set up its own three-man inquiry team of Executive Council members, headed by President Paul Gallagher. They promised that there would be no whitewash. Someone's head seemed likely to roll and Rice was favourite. He was not helped when production staff at Wapping voted to seek a union other than the EETPU to represent them. I had my doubts about the wisdom of establishing the inquiry. I thought it unlikely that the TUC would accept either its independence or its conclusions, and felt it could offer dangerous hostages to fortune.

'The Wapping issue has been an unmitigated disaster. It has given the EETPU's opponents an almost unlimited armoury of weapons upon which to impale us.' That was the colourful opening to the inquiry team's report. The inquiry broadly cleared the union of the allegations of breaking the TUC directives. But Rice was severely criticized for 'a serious error of judgement' and for sailing 'perilously close to the wind'. The inquiry found a technical breach of one directive because of a misunderstanding. Twenty employees were recruited after the TUC instruction not to take such action.

Not surprisingly, Tom Rice opted for early retirement, actually the sacrificial offering to persuade the TUC to close the books. Eric Hammond volunteered further extensive undertakings to limit the union's role at Wapping to the minimum. Our optimists believed that this would be enough to satisfy the TUC, but I was a pessimist. The hounds had tasted blood and would bay for more.

In the midst of this, News International imposed a non-negotiated three-year pay deal at Wapping, with US-style individual employment contracts. Union recognition was further away than ever. The company's Bill O'Neill said: 'The union that would be acceptable to us isn't to the TUC. The unions that would be acceptable to the TUC are unacceptable to us.' The TUC veto on EETPU recognition at Wapping had ensured a non-union establishment.

The TUC again moved against us. It seized on that technical breach to which we had needlessly confessed. There was talk of a three-month suspension for us. But Eric Hammond had done his homework. Once again he warned the TUC of potential legal action to protect our position. His contention was that the TUC lacked power under its rules to punish a subsequent breach of a directive.

By now the union was gravely at odds with the TUC over the vexed issue of the so-called 'no strike' agreements. Hammond claimed that the disciplinary moves over Wapping were intended to 'mute our voice, diminish our influence' during consideration of the strike-free deals, the TUC version of the gagging writ. The TUC General Council voted by twenty-one votes to fourteen to defer action against us so that Norman Willis could get legal advice.

In April 1988 a 2–1 majority of the TUC General Council voted against suspending us and decided instead to censure us strongly. The TUC's lawyers had confirmed Hammond's claim that suspension in the circumstances would break the TUC's own rules. Censure was of little consequence, but the tension grew over strike-free agreements. The mood on our Executive Council, smarting at the TUC's snub to our inquiry report, was defiant.

The TUC censure did no real damage to the EETPU. But it was an attempt to humiliate us and was unprecedented. So was our reaction. Again we contended that the TUC had flouted its own rule-book. Eric Hammond told the General Council: 'We will not co-operate with an inadmissible penalty under the rules.' The TUC ordered the full EETPU Executive Council to attend its next meeting for the censure to be formally administered. Our Executive Council reply was a prompt and unanimous turndown. By then though, we had already set in motion action over strike-free deals which led inexorably to our departure from the TUC's ranks.

Long-term results of the Wapping dispute

The battle over Wapping heralded a long-awaited breakthrough for the entire national newspaper industry and busted an indefensible labour relations system. It produced one clear victor: Rupert Murdoch. He knew the time to kick the unions – when they were down. It was draconian, but this wearisome and malignant dispute also crudely highlighted the enormity of the divide between the old-fashioned Left unionism of Scargill, the print unions and their like, and the new-style, market-orientated unionism which the electricians boldly proclaimed on its merits.

After the miners' strike, and after Wapping, there could be no doubt of the direction which the unions had to take to survive. The EETPU's behaviour over Wapping was flawed. The union made no material long-term gains of consequence in what was really a fight over territory and power. But more and more unions now tread the co-operative path with management in an industrial atmosphere of revived employer ascendancy. The EETPU was the first to make a virtue of necessity. As usual, the rest, grudgingly, shamefacedly, follow on.

I mourn Fleet Street, warts and all. It had character, panache and could be splendidly irresponsible. Its pubs were our clubs. The rivalry, the ribaldry, the gossip, the camaraderie, is all dispersed. It is not a place for newspapermen, past or present, to visit any more. What the Luftwaffe's wartime bombs failed to do, the predatory print unions eventually achieved. They brashly shrugged off warning after warning of terminal decline, and they scorned all reform until it was too late. They handed Fleet Street over to the Hooray Henries, to the smart young advertising, building society and insurance executives, to the accountants, to the lawyers, who are today's inhabitants. If Murdoch

152

was the willing undertaker in Fleet Street's burial, it was the unions that supplied the corpse. They killed it off, and they have no alibi.

11

Independent Union

The first TUC conference which I attended, and reported, was in 1961. Ted Hill, the TUC President, announced the expulsion of the electricians' union from the TUC. Hill, a crumple-faced and good-humoured old Cockney boilermaker (later a lord), said: 'It is with profound regret that I have to ask the ETU delegation to withdraw from Congress and surrender their credentials.' His regret was real, for he was a friend of the disgraced Communist regime, the ETU ballot-riggers.

Twenty-seven years on – at what seemed sure to be my last TUC gathering – I was there as part of the electricians' delegation to witness the union's second expulsion from the TUC.

Those two TUC judgements, so many years apart, were for very different offences. The first was a consequence of a massive fraud that swindled the ordinary members out of their democratic rights, while the second was due to the EETPU's refusal to accept two binding awards of the TUC's inter-union disputes committee.

Yet there was a solid bridge between them. The old TUC establishment did next to nothing to help uncover that original Communist plot. After their epic High Court victory, the union's new anti-Communist leaders were treated as mavericks and undesirables in TUC circles. They were branded and never forgiven for exposing a scandal that rubbed off on all unions and was a body-blow to the Left extremists. Ever since, the electricians' leaders have faced personal vilification from the distortion of their aims by the trade union Left. The EETPU position is still damned, regardless of the merits of the case, and EETPU arguments, however reasoned, are scorned for their source, not their content.

The outcry over strike-free deals was the classic example. The 1988 expulsion from the TUC, ostensibly over these agreements, was the culmination of the long-running campaign against the union's moderate command.

Not that the union was forced into a corner. Even its few trade union friends found it difficult to defend its unapologetic and pugnacious posture. Some tried. They aimed to promote a false unity through woolly compromise that might be sold by the unprincipled to the uninformed.

The EETPU leadership, obstinate and truculent, was not unprincipled, and it reflected the views of its membership. As the pressure on the union mounted, so did its defiance. It balloted its members to see if they would back the stand on strike-free deals, though the price was almost certain to be exclusion from the TUC.

In numerous newspaper articles Eric Hammond drummed out our message: that we would not be bullied into tearing up our agreements in response to unjustified TUC demands. We used our own journal, *Contact*, sent by post to every member at their homes, to underline the gravity of the Executive Council's recommendation for a rule change that would provide for TUC affiliation only if the union was free to make the agreements it wanted. Our front page carried a bold 'Vote "Yes" ' headline. My editorial claimed that 'the TUC is in the grip of those whose inward-looking, class-based ideology has been instrumental in the steady decline of the British trade union movement.' Inside the paper, Eric Hammond declared: 'We must give the TUC, indeed the nation, an unmistakeable message – that we stand for a modern, independent union, accountable to its members and free to make agreements of their choosing.'

I produced a hard-hitting booklet, entitled *The Price of Freedom*, which spelled out the long-term history and the contemporary background to the dispute. It concluded: 'Once again the TUC is about to shoot itself in the foot. Its latest and perhaps worst-ever self-inflicted wound – our enforced exit – is likely to leave it crippled and obsolete for the foreseeable future.'

The EETPU conducted sample surveys of its members which showed overwhelming backing for strike-free deals, with binding arbitration, and roundly opposed any TUC diktat. Wapping was an inexpedient battlefield for a showdown with the TUC, but the EETPU now had no such inhibitions. Its stance was open and unequivocal, and it advocated the new-style agreements on their merits, not as deals cooked up with the bosses to secure recognition – as its opponents alleged.

The ballot produced a 5–1 majority for the rule change. There was a 43 per cent return from the 358,959 ballot papers issued – the second highest poll in the union's history. There were 128,400 (83.33 per cent) for the change and 25,680 (16.67 per cent) against it. It was, said a jubilant Eric Hammond, 'a declaration of independence by our members'.

Strike-free deals: Orion and Christian Salvesen

The simmering crisis had earlier come to a head over complaints to the TUC Disputes Committee about strike-free agreements signed by the EETPU at two greenfield sites – with Orion, a Japanese-owned television plant, and Christian Salvesen, a distribution complex. We had seen off competition from other unions to win the agreements, and our defeated rivals squealed. The TUC ordered us to break the agreements with the companies. We were instructed to expel our Christian Salvesen members, including those who were never before in any union. It would have been an extraordinary bonus for non-unionism. However, we refused to accept the TUC rulings, declaring that we would honour our bargains with the employers and with our members.

The TUC's Special Review Body threatened a virtual ban on all strike-free deals. The cant of our critics was revealed when we published a damning list of agreements containing binding arbitration clauses, some of them made by our most vociferous opponents, including the TGWU, GMBATU, SOGAT and the NGA. We spotlighted the GMBATU, a complainant against us over Christian Salvesen, and persistently hostile. The GMBATU's supreme humbug was to subsequently sign an almost identical agreement for another Christian Salvesen depot.

That June, the union held its industrial conference at Scarborough. The series of industry-based gatherings, spread over the week, were made up of shop stewards, local branch officials and other elected activists. Eric Hammond used the separate conferences as another platform from which to expose the TUC's organized hypocrisy. He made it plain that the EETPU, sure to be suspended and then expelled, would only return to the TUC on the basis of free and autonomous unions. He emphasized that he spoke from some strength. Our finances were up £2.5 million to £16.9 million, and membership had risen by 2,000 in the first half of the year. Moreover, he said that if plans went ahead to merge with the AEU the EETPU would not re-enter the TUC by the backdoor as part of the new organization, but would be more likely to force the engineers out of the TUC altogether.

Meanwhile, at Congress House in London, the TUC's reviewers took another look at the draft code of practice for single-union, strike-free deals. The review body was supposed to concentrate on defining the role of the unions in the nineties. Instead, its work was dominated by the strike-free affair, thanks mainly to the need to appease the TGWU, the largest affiliate, which wanted an outright ban. (The TGWU even allowed its crass prejudice to block a £40 million new Ford plant at Dundee where the AEU was poised to make such a deal. As it turned out, the Spanish got the factory, and the much-needed jobs.) The review body grappled with the overall problem of the strike-free agreements. It was a measure of the prevailing hypocrisy that some unions, which had officially pressed for a ban, in practice carried on signing what amounted to strike-free deals with employers.

We could see that the big general workers' unions were out to write a new TUC charter which would greatly increase their powers and authority. John (the Walrus) Edmonds, of the GMBATU, emerged as leader of the pack, predicting four big super-unions by the end of the century. It was a cynical exercise, as unions based on a craft, occupation or even industry, would go. TUC-regimented 'spheres of influence' would mostly allow the giant general unions to recruit freely while the rest would be confined to the narrowest possible base. General workers' unions could continue to take in electricians. The EETPU could recruit no one else.

Eric Hammond attacked this unprecedented onslaught on union sovereignty in an attempt to awaken and galvanize the middle-sized and smaller unions that would be swallowed up in the process. It was, he said, merger by menace, and therefore unacceptable.

The review body finalized its code. The revised version left little room for further strike-free deals and was tougher than the original draft, thanks to pressure from the Left. Hammond's response was that the EETPU would stick to its chosen path 'even if that means breaking every rule in the TUC book'.

TUC priorities were clear. On the day it decided to polarize attitudes by virtually outlawing agreements that could aid recruitment, it also announced that total membership of TUC-affiliated unions in the year ending 31 December 1987 had dropped to 9,126,911 – a fall of 116,386. Curiously, as membership haemorrhaged, the TUC barons were more concerned to open new wounds than to staunch the outflow.

On the eve of the TUC General Council meeting which would suspend it, the EETPU published details of two more single-union, strike-free deals, and talked of another ten in the pipeline.

Suspension of the EETPU

Eric Hammond and Paul Gallagher travelled from our Scarborough conference to represent us at the TUC meeting. (I went along too, mainly to handle the media interest that we expected.) On Hammond's briefcase, a sticker cheekily invited: 'Put a spark in your life. Love an electrician.' Not where we were going, they wouldn't. There was no hint of contrition in Hammond's fifty-five-minute speech to an acrimonious TUC General Council. He accepted that the EETPU had broken the rules and must take the consequences. Nevertheless, he turned on the Council to contend that it was the TUC that should be in the dock for bringing the movement into disrepute. He accused the TGWU, GMBATU and NUPE (the public employees' union) of plotting against the EETPU. He went on to claim that the unions had saddled Labour with unpopular policies. Norman Willis argued that the clash was not about strike-free deals, but 'about whether one union can loot in a field where another is established. If they can it's a sad day for British industrial relations. It's anarchy,' he said.

There were sharp exchanges across the table. Hammond and Gallagher left before the predetermined outcome. We were given two weeks to scrap our two deals or be suspended. The vote was thirty-six to four, with the AEU's Bill Jordan leading the tiny minority. He declared the meeting 'a shambles'.

Press comment was heavily in our favour. The Labour-supporting *Daily Mirror* said: 'Even Mr Tebbit couldn't have injured the trade unions as much as they mutilated themselves yesterday.' The right-wing *Sun* said: 'Outside the TUC, the electricians can find freedom.'

Back in Scarborough our Executive Council held an emergency session. There was unanimous rejection of the two-week deadline. It would be ten days after the expiry date before our membership ballot would be completed. We would not pre-empt that. There was an on-the-spot symptom of support for the leadership when our engineering industry members at the conference voted by 160–2 in favour of sticking to our strike-free deals.

The EETPU had suggested to the TUC that where unions compete for membership, the workforce should settle the matter by ballot. The union put this point once more, but got nowhere with the TUC, which reported that 'if it became the practice to seek workers' views, it would be difficult to resist the claim of such views to be paramount.'

The two weeks grace brought no change. The suspension was automatic.

The EETPU's 5–1 ballot result was the decisive demonstration of rank-and-file support which it sought. The only debate on the Executive Council was over whether we should bother to exercise our right of appeal at the forthcoming Congress or should quit the TUC immediately, thus saving £160,000 in affiliation fees. The ultimate consensus was that we should attend Congress and maximize our public impact. We would not go quietly. We had consistently said that we did not wish to leave the TUC. We would be seen to go the last mile. But we would not shift our position. The TUC, notorious for last-minute vacillation and ambivalence, could expect no help from the EETPU.

The TUC General Council confirmed that suspension would become expulsion at the September Congress. Only representatives from the AEU, engaged in prolonged merger talks with the EETPU, and from the CPSA (the civil servants' union), opposed our marching orders. AEU President Bill Jordan warned that our expulsion would lead to an 'all-out war' between trade unionists which would be highly damaging to the movement. Norman Willis countered that the EETPU had rejected its obligations to the TUC and to other unions. 'You don't play fast and loose with the rules,' he said. I retorted publicly for the union that there would be no membership war of our choosing, but we would 'resist and retaliate' if we were raided.

Trial

A fortnight before the Congress, the General Council agreed arrangements for our 'trial'. They were anxious to minimize the fuss and damage from the accompanying media jamboree. Acres of newsprint and plenty of prime-time television were guaranteed. They knew that we would win public support in an open and untrammelled debate which allowed us to argue beyond the specific issue of obedience to TUC decisions and to put the wider case for strike-free deals. There was a foolish and abortive move on the part of the Left to conduct the trial behind closed doors. It was agreed instead to hurry the debate through on the opening morning of the Bournemouth conference. Norman Willis would have fifteen minutes to prosecute, Eric Hammond would have twenty minutes to appeal, with a further five minutes for Willis to sum up. The whole messy business could thus be condensed into less than forty-five minutes, all at the outset of the conference, rather than overshadow the whole week. A swift and clean excision was the best that the TUC could hope for in the circumstances.

Already the dangers of a vicious recruitment war were emerging. Our principal rivals drew up their battle plans, ready to act against us as soon as we were outside the TUC and the protection of the TUC's 1939 Bridlington agreement, which prohibits unions from poaching each others' members. Norman Willis tried to cool the temperature somewhat, claiming that there was no passion for 'some sort of bloodbath'.

But there was. Unions such as the TGWU and Manufacturing, Science and Finance, both under left-wing leadership, together with the GMBATU, were raring to go for our membership. A left-wing breakaway body for disgruntled EETPU members was set up, and bragged that special 'holding' branches of other TUC-affiliated unions would take in and offer services to our members, prior to their eventual transfer to a new TUC-backed union for electricians and plumbers.

We were, though, less concerned by these overt activities than by the possibility of employers getting cold feet. They might well try to exclude us from joint negotiations where other unions agitated against us.

If, however, the Bridlington agreement would offer us no further protection, neither were we bound by it. We recruited hard, especially in the white-collar area. Single-union deals, where we represented all grades of worker at a plant, blurred the old boundaries, turned us increasingly into a general union and presented limitless opportunities for expansion.

We were about to be hanged and it concentrated our minds wonderfully. We drew up a rough and ready balance sheet. It was evident that the trade union movement was in no shape to talk about runaway winners or losers. De-unionization was well under way as new employers refused to recognize unions and, here and there, existing recognition agreements were unilaterally scrapped. Nor was there any rush by workers to join organizations seen by potential recruits to be more concerned with their own in-fighting than with promoting the best interests of their members.

We reckoned that we could come out of the inter-union conflict with a credit balance, with membership gains. In the economic and industrial climate of the day, that would be no mean achievement. At least our brand of new realism and our fresh approach to the aspirations of a modern workforce gave us far greater appeal than that of the exponents of the old class-war divisions perpetuated by the trade union conservatives.

Few people cared about the TUC's views on the poll tax, nationalization, defence or foreign policy. Thatcherism had seen to that. We were prepared to stay inside a reformist TUC camp, but were unlikely to miss the fatuous and semi-defunct institution we were leaving behind. The industrial activities, including contact with government, which could directly affect our members could and would be pursued by us independently.

The Bournemouth conference

On the eve of the Bournemouth conference, opinion polls in the *Sunday Times* and *Sunday Telegraph* suggested broad support for our style of trade unionism among trade unionists and among the public. Surprisingly, despite the brawls and discord, there was a high level of public support for unions generally, something that was not reflected in the falling membership roll.

Our delegation arrived at our Bournemouth hotel, knowing that we would only need our rooms for a couple of nights. Our Executive Council met on the Sunday. We heard about a late flurry of activity, with a tentative move from Norman Willis and a plea from Bill Jordan for us to think again. It was all pie in the sky.

We planned to hang on to the public relations initiative which we had mostly maintained throughout the dispute. We agreed on a disciplined withdrawal by our delegation immediately the expulsion debate speeches were over, rather than be drummed out by the formal and predetermined vote.

The *Guardian* ran a pre-conference profile of me by its Labour Editor, Keith Harper, who said that my experience, both as politician and as journalist 'has considerably helped the EETPU to parcel its package to the public in a way most unions would envy'. He added: 'He has become indispensable to the electricians' propaganda machine, carrying his mission with as much zest as his old colleague, Mr Bernard Ingham, does at Downing Street.'

He reported that there were those who thought that because of my prominence in the SDP, I would be quite happy for the EETPU to be permanently outside the TUC and expelled from the Labour Party, too. He quoted me: 'I have never been in favour of us coming out of the TUC but we aren't going to accept the rules of the club as they are at the moment.' It was a fair summary. I had been too close to the trade unions for too long either to work for or welcome the split, but I was entirely in step with the union – the EETPU could not stay in at any price.

On the Monday morning, prior to the conference, we had a quick meeting of our twenty-one delegates, then walked down the hill from the hotel to the conference centre. Outside the conference centre there were as many demonstrators against the government's Employment Training Scheme as there were against the EETPU. We got in without incident, and were allocated three rows of seats on the far right at the back. Television cameras had tracked us all morning and the journalists were mob-handed.

Norman Willis was melancholic, not surprisingly, since his task was to move the General Council's recommendation to expel us. His demeanour suggested that all this hurt him far more than it hurt the EETPU. I think that it did. He said that to give a union licence to unilaterally decide which parts of Bridlington it accepted or rejected would make a mockery of the term 'trade union movement'.

Eric Hammond's trip to the microphone was accompanied by an uncanny and unusual silence. The Left had responded to the tactical need for restraint. They accepted the TUC leadership's appeal to cut the customary abuse of the man they knew loved them to hate him. Even a typical pugnacious and uncompromising speech failed to provoke the habitual storm of booing and jeers, and was delivered in near silence.

The EETPU's expulsion, Hammond said, would give union members a choice between the future and the past. He believed that they would 'choose freedom as our members have chosen independence'. He was not there to appeal or say 'sorry' but 'to tell you and beyond you the British people, why you are expelling my union'. He made an eleventh-hour peace proposal – for the TUC to agree to allow workers at Orion and Christian Salvesen to vote on whether the EETPU should accept the two disputes committee awards. 'Our movement faces an ever-widening split. Our hand reaches out before the gap becomes too great. . . . Will you do the same, will you let the members decide?'

162

Why not? It was reasonable. It was faultless logic. It was also a pious hope with no prospect of assent. Hammond knew that the TUC was far too far up the disciplinary road to allow for a ploy which could only have one outcome – victory for the EETPU. Our members at the companies concerned would have backed us firmly in any dispute. Once again however, the proposition wrong-footed the TUC. It was good public relations on a day when we had to look to the wider audience away from the narrow confines of the conference.

Eric threw the book at the indoctrinated assembly. He rubbed in our members' enthusiasm for the market system and its values 'that infuriates the sherry party revolutionaries with their model resolutions and conference-hall rhetoric' who failed to reflect their members' views. He alleged victimization and a 'claque of intolerance' by the General Council majority.

Norman Willis, in reply, scoffed at the idea that the EETPU had been the victim of a witch-hunt. He said: 'This has not been a matter of Left and Right. It has been a matter of right and wrong and you have ended up in the wrong.' Nothing Hammond had said, he added, could change the expulsion recommendation.

Expulsion

This time, then, the TUC would not blink. It was all we needed to know. Eric got up from his seat and, as arranged, our delegation was on its feet and on its way. As we left the hall it was akin to a rugby scrum. Photographers and TV cameramen jostled and shoved to get their shots. Inside the hall, the vote for our expulsion was overwhelming. Only the AEU and half the CPSA delegation voted against it.

I had fixed a press conference at the hotel. Eric Hammond held court. He made it clear that 'The Independent Union' was now in operation and would recruit with vigour. 'From journalists to janitors, no one will be told to go back through the open door', he pledged. He ridiculed the breakaway electricians' group as 'Left-led quislings'.

The next morning's slabs of newsprint did well by us. The *Mirror* trumpeted that 'the break came because the TUC puts rules above its members and the electricians' leader, Eric Hammond, puts his members above any TUC rules'. This was a pro-Labour view. The leftish *Guardian* argued that the TUC was right to kick us out 'on the narrow but substantive issue', but in doing so had 'shot itself in the foot again just when it desperately needs to improve its image and reality'.

The *Financial Times* said that the electricians 'have skilfully presented themselves as the modern union . . . the TUC is widely regarded as a troglodyte organisation'. The *Independent* thought the TUC rules were not applied to us with relevance or fairness. And the *Express* said that Eric Hammond 'spoke up for millions of rank-and-file trade unionists'.

The Communist *Morning Star* sneered that we were the toast of the media – except for the *Morning Star*. It was right about that anyway, as the *Star* slated us and said that the EETPU should now be booted out of the Labour Party.

There was plenty to think over as I drove home from Bournemouth later that day. The EETPU had taken an enormous gamble – calculated, but no less a gamble for that – and was now on its own. It was free to build its organization without TUC-imposed constraints and free to put the £300,000-plus annual TUC affiliation fee to good use on behalf of its members.

The EETPU was not out to establish an alternative trade union centre to the TUC, though that could not be ruled out if the AEU joined forces with it. What made much more sense was a bid to draw in the non-TUC professional and managerial staff associations under the EETPU umbrella. Eric Hammond had appointed Roy Sanderson to succeed Tom Rice at the head of our white-collar section. Sanderson, one-time top Communist, was nowadays a known admirer of both Margaret Thatcher and David Owen. He was primarily responsible for negotiating the first company-based, single-union, strike-free deal at Toshiba in Owen's Plymouth constituency. He had served for many years as the union's engineering industry leader, and was convinced that our TUC exit would enable him to push up our membership, as more and more white-collar groups recognized the economies of scale to be gained, either through merger with us or by retaining their basic autonomy in a close working relationship. Our competitive, pragmatic, market-orientated unionism, and our moderation, would appeal strongly to these politically unsullied organizations, which were naturally averse to the politicized TUC unions, such as the tub-thumping Left-led TGWU and MSF, or the GMBATU, with its pale-pink complexion.

Such organizations could buy into the full range of our services – training, legal, financial and so on. They could make use of our £6 million country mansion at Buxted Park, Sussex, for holiday or weekend breaks, for meetings and conferences. The purchase of the 312-acre estate, a former Arab-owned health farm, was the biggest property deal negotiated by any British union, and was one more symbol of Eric Hammond's entrepreneurial enthusiasm. The huge investment caused some misgivings among Executive Council members but Hammond was sure that it was money well spent. It was certainly one more attraction in the EETPU recruitment shop window.

There was a downside, of course. We expected an unsavoury politically-led war against us. Those who would bear the brunt were not the national level policy-makers but ordinary members and especially our local officials and shop stewards. No one knew whether they would be ostracized by their counterparts in other unions or whether disputes would break out in joint negotiating bodies.

Nor could we be satisfied that our overall organization was adequately manned or equipped to take on everything that the TUC unions collectively might throw at us. Not that the TUC was in much condition to be effective. Our first-day expulsion was the worst possible start to its Bournemouth week. It went on to register a series of imbecilic decisions: to boycott the government's Employment Training programme; to phase out all nuclear power; to reaffirm support for unilateral nuclear disarmament; to call for the repeal of all Conservative industrial relations legislation, including that on ballots. What a congress! What a shower!

The EETPU and Labour

Labour's annual conference was imminent. I had no particular personal concern about the union's relationship with the Labour Party. I thought the link justified, but incestuous. What I had to recognize was how much that link meant to many EETPU members, some of them firm friends and supporters of the union's leadership. It was important not to alienate them and open up needless divisions within the EETPU ranks.

The *Morning Star* was not alone in demanding that Labour acted. Both John Prescott and Eric Heffer, contesting with the incumbent Roy Hattersley for the party's deputy leadership, were hostile to us. Prescott, with uncharacteristic caution, suggested that there should be no precipitate moves, but Heffer wanted the immediate removal of the EETPU.

Only unions recognized by the TUC as *bona fide* can affiliate to Labour. Eric Hammond let it be known that we would fight in the courts any attempt to expel us from the Labour Party. Our legal advice was that a TUC ruling that we were not *bona fide*, sure to conflict with the views of the trade union Certification Officer, would be set aside. We had used the courts successfully to force the Scottish TUC to recognize that it had no constitutional power to suspend us in Scotland. Thus we were legally prepared to fight this issue.

Labour's Left pressed for our ejection, but Neil Kinnock was privately opposed to any such action. He was unwilling to lose the EETPU's voting strength when our support was valuable in his efforts to push Labour towards moderation and so to make it electable. The EETPU had a more sophisticated political structure, geared to ensuring that moderation prevailed, than any other Labour-affiliated union. A confidential survey for Labour estimated that there were only about 4,000 politically active trade unionists in Labour's ranks throughout the country, out of some six million potential members in Labour-affiliated unions. The EETPU undoubtedly had more than its fair share of those activists.

A public dogfight over expulsion, with resultant victory for the Left, would be another serious blow to Labour's recovery prospects. There was also the not inconsiderable matter of the EETPU's sizeable cash contribution to the hard-up party. Not surprisingly, the party's National Executive Committee decided that we retained the right to affiliate. There was a brief attempt at the conference to challenge this verdict, but it was firmly quashed. Labour's pragmatism has since ensured that the union's expulsion has vanished from the agenda.

The EETPU and the AEU: failure to merge

Now came a major setback to those who hoped that we would join up with the AEU to create a right-wing super-union. Both union leaderships were divided, but it was the AEU which had the biggest internal problems. Common sense dictated that it should jettison its fossilized structure and many of its practices, but it was all too much for the AEU traditionalists. There were problems too, over who might get the top jobs in an amalgamated set-up. The AEU President Bill Jordan was a merger enthusiast, whereas General Secretary Gavin Laird was a decided sceptic. The edgy relationship between the two of them was no help to progress. The AEU Left was fiercely antagonistic, seeing the right-wing electricians as a threat to its existence. The AEU anti-mergerists used the EETPU non-TUC status as a point of issue against amalgamation.

I regarded the question of a merger with some indifference. On a

166

personal level, I would not be around to see it happen. On a practical level, a merger might assist in our recruitment struggle, and economies of scale could prove useful, but AEU cobwebs would not lightly blow away. We would be tied in to a long-standing ramshackle outfit which, despite Laird's reformist efforts, lacked both the organizational and financial disciplines which the EETPU had built up over the years. Another drawback was the disruptive AEU Left, which always threatened, and sometimes succeeded.

The two leaderships were spared further problematical negotiations when the AEU's policy-making National Committee voted narrowly against merger. Jordan recorded his disgust, and he and Laird wrote to us to express their disappointment. Laird's reservations were the subject of comment when the AEU letter came before our Executive Council, one member suggesting that Laird had in fact personally engineered the failure.

The EETPU celebrated its hundredth anniversary with a centenary policy conference in Jersey. The 809 delegates voted massively in support of our stand at the TUC 'in defence of the independence of our union and the rights of the individual members of all trade unions'. There were no second thoughts. It underlined the unity of the Executive Council, the full-time officials, the elected delegates and the overall membership.

State of the EETPU since 1989

I had reckoned to spend up to five years with the EETPU, and I had now spent five and a half years. During that time, I had seen through significant changes in its communications, and had been involved in historic happenings which had led to the trade union map being partly redrawn. It had been a rumbustious, sometimes frustrating, but always invigorating, period in my life. Now it was time to go.

Since I left my union post in mid-1989, changes on the union front have been less than dramatic, and there has been something of a stalemate. The all-out membership war did not materialize, rather, border skirmishes have been the order of the day. The union has continued to sign single-union, strike-free deals, but they still cover less than a tenth of the total membership.

That overall membership is much the same as it was a couple of years earlier – something not to be sneezed at, at a time when most unions are contracting and unemployment is rising. The EETPU has made particular advances through its renamed white-collar section, the Federation of Professional Associations, which now embraces a remarkable range of occupations, including professional divers, senior probation officers, journalists, nuclear supervisors, steel industry managers, power-loom overlookers, Ministry of Defence staff and fire officers, to name but a few.

The breakaway electricians' organization has flopped and Left influence within the EETPU has steadily dwindled to insignificance. On the shopfloor, working relationships with members of other unions have mostly stayed intact. Disputes directly related to the EETPU's non-TUC status have been few. Our representatives mostly sit alongside those of TUC-affiliated unions on joint negotiating bodies, as before. And an EETPU merger with the AEU is back on the agendas of both organizations.

It would be facile to pronounce the EETPU a model union, but it contrasts sharply with the singular lack of vision and statesmanship within the TUC, where the dismal antics of the big battalions combine to highlight the gulf between the leaders and the led. The EETPU favours growth and profitability as the best means to guarantee its members' job security. It is ballot-based and populist. Its strike-free deals, rejection of the class war, together with its brand of business unionism offer a coherent and practical approach with which ordinary trade unionists everywhere can identify. Its provision of benefits and services are a deliberate recognition of its members as consumers.

It has certainly not foresworn the strike weapon, which it uses in many industries and the Executive Council approves a crop of pre-strike ballots at every meeting. Three-quarters of those ballots endorse industrial action but it is seldom needed once employers know that the union and its members, acting democratically and within the law, mean business. That said, the EETPU openly advocates co-operation, rather than conflict, as the way forward. That too, is in tune with the views of most trade unionists today, including shop stewards, all less militant than before in the post-Thatcher era of recession and tough employment laws.

Quite simply, the EETPU is leaving other unions behind in its readiness to change in a fast-moving industrial world. It accepts that skilled workers, with middle-class values and middle-class mortgages, are not tailor-made trade unionists. They must be wooed and won over.

The union's new realism has had its impact in Britain's boardrooms. The union has first-hand examples of a new phenomenon – company squabbles over whether or not to sign single-union deals. Personnel directors see the advantages of a structured two-way communication with employees to resolve grievances and reduce staff turnover. The union is the relevant channel. However, managing directors and other board members are generally less sympathetic, and increasingly they opt for no union at all. More than one personnel director has quit from frustration over this.

The union knows that if it turns to a more traditional campaign to win members and company recognition it risks plant closures, especially where overseas employers are concerned. Foreign companies, particularly newcomers to Britain, are often anti-union and are ready to lean on employees or to bribe them with improved pay packets to keep their plants union-free. Other unions which have encountered this resistance have gone for single-union deals, sometimes accepting in the process inferior terms and conditions to those for the industry generally, in order to secure agreements.

It is an indication of the poverty of vision of British management that so few employers remain prepared to embrace the strike-free agreement, fearing encroachment on their managerial prerogative and preferring to slug it out in a dispute.

The EETPU and other issues

The EETPU's championship of taboo causes and revisionist heresies has been doughtily consistent. It includes support for Polish Solidarity when the TUC was hostile, opposition to Scargill's undemocratic miners' strike, initiating union moves to take ballot money from the government, a pro-EEC posture and hostility to unilateral nuclear disarmament. All these terrible sins are now respectable in TUC eyes. The EETPU backs electoral reform and one-member, one-vote, within the Labour Party – policies which are gaining ground all the time. Even those strike-free deals appear to find an echo in the TUC-supported European Social Charter, which allows people to join the union of their choice.

In the edition of *Contact*, the EETPU newspaper, which I edited just before I bowed out, I wrote a farewell message which said: 'The union is certainly not fault-free. But if trade unions are to survive and prosper in the interests of their members and hopefully of the wider community, then they will need to follow broadly the trail which the EETPU has blazed.' It is a sentiment which I still endorse.

169

12

In Their Hands

The trade union movement, whether it realizes it or not, is rapidly approaching a crisis. The 1991 TUC annual conference was the thirteenth under the Conservatives who have done so much to provoke the unions' self-destructive tendencies. In 1990 TUC-affiliated membership fell to 8.15 million, compared with 12.1 million in 1979, and 1991's prolonged recession, with its impact on jobs, seems sure to drag the total TUC membership well below the eight million mark. The TUC, heading for a £1.2 million deficit in 1992, has sought to cut its costs by closing down committees, and by reducing staffing levels.

And worse is possibly to come, as yet another batch of legislative changes proposed by the government threatens a further fall in membership, mainly through a plan to compel unions to secure the explicit written agreement of individual workers to have their union dues automatically 'checked off' by employers from their pay packets.

Future of the TUC

As union membership spirals downwards, demands grow for the TUC's Congress House headquarters to reduce itself still further to an information, research and service centre. The super-unions on the near horizon can then assume the TUC's traditional role as lobbyists, policy-makers and occasional inter-union arbitrators. This makes a lot of sense for the large general unions. It adds greatly to their powers of patronage and steps up the pressure on the smaller unions to shelter within the encircling embrace of their bigger brothers. The same major unions, however, already run their own information, research and service operations. They are unlikely to scrap them as they grow bigger still through strong-arm takeovers, and they will be reluctant to subscribe to the TUC for duplicated resources – resources which, if maintained, can only help to preserve the unwelcome independence of the smaller fry. The TUC, its assets stripped, will have scant reason to exist at all.

It is a dismal prospect for those who retain a soft spot for that lumbering old TUC carthorse. It may never raise another gallop, but it is premature to kill it off. This is not said from mere sentiment – the TUC's unfortunate recent past rules that out.

The TUC is the sum of its parts. The would-be assassins are the same big unions who, browbeating the central organization and using it to pursue their vested interests, have brought it to its present state of sickness. Their dominance has been markedly counter-productive for trade unionists' best interests. Absolute power to the big unions would corrupt them absolutely.

It was the leaders of those unions, not the TUC functionaries, whose wretched behaviour gave Mrs Thatcher her excuse to ignore any collectively representative workers' voice, flawed or not, and to portray the unions as undemocratic would-be law-breakers, out of touch with ordinary members' views. It was those same union barons who subsequently engineered the injurious bust-up with the EETPU.

Mrs Thatcher took every advantage of union deficiencies. Unions had no place in the ideal world of Finchley Woman. She missed few tricks in her sustained campaign to break them, and her rigorous legal restraints on them remain high among the measures most favoured by the public in her comprehensive legislative programme. The unions offer no apparent reason for Mr Major to bring them in from the cold.

It is all a far cry from the early post-war years when governments of differing political colours worked with the unions on a reciprocal basis. Now the TUC gazes wistfully through the Whitehall letterbox at the corridors of power along which it once strutted. Tripartism, with government, employers and unions together deciding the nation's destiny, is long dead. Here and there union worthies sit on such bodies as the National Economic Development Council, but no one pretends that ministers listen to them.

The TUC lacks firm leadership, and Congress House is a citadel without a cause. Bevin, Deakin, Williamson, Lawther, Cousins, Jones – great names from the TUC's past – all wielded huge authority through their personalities as well as their block votes. They were authoritarian but they could usually deliver. The sixties found the TUC bureaucracy led by Woodcock, the thinking man's trade unionist, then by the shrewd and humorous fixer, Feather. Murray, next in line, was in the Woodcock mould. Each of them battled against adversity, but each gave the TUC stature. Today's embattled incumbent, the affable but undistinguished Norman Willis, is subjected to whispering union critics who sneer that those whom he fails to confuse, don't understand him. They have a point but the rotund Willis has no heavyweight General Council back-up in the struggle for progress and reform.

The aimlessness cannot be hidden. Workers see no purpose or advantage in union membership, and consequently vote with their feet. That trend has been grievously accelerated by recession and particularly by the erosion of manufacturing industry. The accompanying expansion of the mostly non-unionized service sector is no compensation.

If Conservative government continues, not only the TUC's future but that of all the unions is bleak. They will remain as outcasts. Yet the big unions betray a lack of confidence in Labour's prospects, which contradicts all the official union hype about the Labour Party as an alternative government. They must make up their minds, as Labour in office would find it essential to deal with a single representative trade union voice, just as sensible employers usually prefer to channel workforce problems through the unions rather than deal piecemeal with a welter of individual grievances. Downgrading the TUC cannot square with Labour's needs, and the party leadership should say so.

It would be an exaggeration to describe today's TUC as fully representative but it is the only central representative body which the mass of trade unionists have got. No wise government would wish to consult, let alone negotiate with, a series of unions, one by one. Would Labour welcome separate talks with the Left-led TGWU, MSF, NALGO or NUPE? With the AEU? With a multiplicity of middle and minnow-sized outfits? In that absurd situation, even the go-it-alone electricians, currently best placed to converse with the government, would be relegated to take their place in a near-static queue.

Labour's roots are in the unions, and the party depends on union money. Union votes still control the party conference. It suits Neil Kinnock, just now, to proclaim a relationship in which the party, not its union paymasters, rules the roost. He openly and properly slapped down Arthur Scargill's pretentious demands for special favours for the unions under Labour. Kinnock knows that the unions have nowhere else to go, that he need not fawn or genuflect, that their hopes are pinned on him to legitimize them again. He would undoubtedly restore some union credit but his concessions would require a quid pro quo. A Labour government would be in desperate need of just about the only kind of help that the unions might usefully provide – on the pay front.

There is a gaping hole in Labour's hesitant and highly unsatisfactory economic policy, in the shape of wage inflation. Brave words about a reshaped relationship with the unions cannot obscure the reason for this conspiracy of silence: fear of union reaction. Incomes policy, the unmentionable phrase, is always with us. Sometime, Labour will be compelled to spell out the dirty words, and so face a bitterly hostile union reaction.

No government which seeks to maintain low inflation, high employment and high growth, can do so without an incomes policy, structured or unstructured. The dilemma is that each incomes policy contains the seeds of its own destruction. The present government's version, Thatcherite or Majorette, is well tried and pretty much unvaried. Fiscal and monetary control reduces output, raises unemployment and thus inhibits the free collective bargainers. Covert application in the public sector aims to push pay settlements below the going inflation rate. In practice, this policy has not succeeded. The UK's wage inflation rate has been consistently above that of most of Britain's major industrial competitors. Britain has suffered from wage inflation and unacceptably high unemployment at the same time.

There is more myth than miracle about the economic triumphs of the past decade, despite Mrs Thatcher's oft-repeated claims, and Prime Minister Major has a lot to explain away. Significant advances under Thatcherism are undeniable. Capitalism has been popularized so that there are now more shareholders than trade unionists. Home-ownership has soared. Industrial relations have been reformed and the attack on restrictive practices has spread, albeit inadequately, to the professions. In a troubled world, Britain is still a good place to live.

But the debit sheet is heavy, too. Resources have switched from the public to the private sector, rather than from rich to poor. Improved living standards are accompanied by a growing deprived underclass. There are unresolved and worsening problems of homelessness, crime, drug-taking and hooliganism. Our littered inner cities are rundown, likewise our vital public services. The recession during 1991 has been deep-seated, and rising unemployment has infiltrated even the customarily affluent regions of the South and South-East. Manufacturing industry is in further sharp decline and bankruptcies pile up.

173

Perhaps most damning of all is the fact that the nation has borrowed to feed consumption rather than to prime the investment that is our future prosperity.

Labour government: the need for a pay policy

In spite of Tory errors, Labour has yet to command the sort of popularity which could bring it into government. Any preference for Labour's social policies, desirably more egalitarian than those of its opponents, is marred by disbelief in its ability to generate the wealth to pay for them. The public still lacks faith in Labour's economic policies and in its managerial competence. Labour today is akin to the poor man's Conservative Party. Its credibility gap has narrowed but is far from bridged, despite Neil Kinnock's belated but severe crackdown on the militants. Its ideas gap is apparent.

Yet the Tories are discredited by recession, by the poll tax fiasco, by their divisions over Europe, and Labour could squeak home by default. If it does so it will once more inherit an economic morass. Wage inflation will loom large. The very arrival of a Labour government will excite pay bargainers, will release pent-up demands, particularly in the public sector where 'catching up' will be seen as legitimate, and will escalate inflation. So too, will high expectations across the field of public spending.

Labour has no answer to wage inflation. Its best shot is a vaguely defined proposal for a national economic assessment, along with unions that tinker nervously and defensively with co-ordinated wage-bargaining machinery to condense the annual pay round. These are tentative advances, but hardly constitute a policy. Labour's commitment to a statutory minimum wage can only add to the inflationary pressures as higher-paid workers insist on retaining their differentials.

Past Labour governments, notably those of 1964 and 1974, have taken office with pay and prices policies which worked, with varying degrees of success, at least in their early post-election periods. Mr Kinnock's cupboard is, however, bare – both in theory and in practice – on the question of prices and incomes. Labour has avoided its homework on pay because it is scared of repudiation by major unions, already denouncing any future wage restraint. It is fearful too, of the past, of previous Labour government failures – failures which objective examination shows were avoidable. Left-of-centre governments can and do successfully operate pay policies (witness the Australian Labour administration's long-running version), and it is an issue which Mr Kinnock needs urgently to address.

A new Labour government would desperately need a breathing space, and could best secure it by courageously ignoring the roars of protest and imposing an immediate temporary prices and incomes freeze of the kind that is explicitly rejected by Prime Minister Major. This would offer the best prospect of forestalling dangerous expectations and should hold the inflation rate at least to that of Britain's EEC neighbours. It should also allow low interest rates, and should protect and create jobs.

Such a move would be far from revolutionary. (We have done it before, as have the French, and even the CBI volunteered a prices freeze in 1970 to try to extricate the Heath government from its difficulties.) A freeze would give a Labour government time to find more permanent solutions. A left-of-centre government must opt for an overt incomes policy for both economic and social reasons. It cannot indulge in the pretence that restraint is not essential, especially for high earners, nor that anomalies would not arise. There can be no freedom from pain and no perfection. Public support is vital, but opinion polls, whatever their shortcomings, have been remarkably consistent in showing that a substantial majority of the public endorse the theory of an incomes policy. They will continue to do so if there is a clear demonstration that an incomes policy is designed to protect real incomes and jobs, and that the alternative is harsh monetary controls which curb output and cause unemployment.

There are fundamentals to any incomes policy, which must comprise a pay norm and price constraint. There must be flexibility to allow for exceptional circumstances – say for low pay or for price rises beyond domestic control. There must be comparability for the public sector with the private sector, and there needs to be an independent institution to administer and arbitrate – something similar to the old Prices and Incomes Board.

The agonizing issue is whether statutory backing is required. I do not believe that exhortation is enough nor that voluntarism, except for brief periods, can work. Voluntarism is a challenge to those who oppose the policy – a challenge that they will soon pick up. If the overall policy is seen to be fair and commands public assent, then sanctions are workable. They must, however, be kept in the background and not used against individuals. (No martyrs, please!) Sanctions might be applied to major companies to prevent inappropriate price increases

175

arising from pay deals which breach agreed criteria. Sanctions could also be used to restrain unions in similar fashion to those in force, but rarely applied, on the industrial relations front. Union immunities would thus be on the line.

There is no available blueprint for an incomes policy, but there is abundant experience, at home and abroad, on which to draw to anticipate the worst pitfalls and to avoid the series of constitutional crises which have dogged past pay policies. Such an approach, post-freeze, should not only prevent a new pay explosion, but should also yield dividends through continuing low inflation and more employment. Trade unions would be in business, not as pay policemen, but to lobby, interpret and negotiate within the guidelines on behalf of their members, probably to a far greater and more effective extent than most of them do at present.

An incomes policy could also address the question of a statutory minimum wage. The principal and very valid argument against a statutory minimum wage so far has been that higher-paid workers would use it as a platform on which to build – with inflationary effect. That argument largely disappears if a statutory minimum wage is an integral part of a justly structured pay policy.

A prices and incomes policy may be regarded as bad politics, but what is Labour's alternative to the Conservative way? Acceptance of the European exchange rate mechanism, lower interest rates, credit controls, the market, are variations on a Tory theme. The use of unemployment as an anti-inflation weapon is a common factor in the circumstances, however much Labour may cavil at the charge. Labour claims that it would manage, not abolish, capitalism. Why should anyone expect Labour to do this better than those with both the experience and the genuine belief in such a system? It is a bizarre proposition which Labour, still hypnotized by the Thatcherite revolution, refuses to acknowledge.

Labour–union relationship

A new Labour government would have a better chance than hitherto of introducing its own policy for incomes, overcoming union reservations and objections. Mrs Thatcher has tamed the unions. Mr Kinnock should try to take them with him, but need not kow-tow to them. Nor, privately, would many union leaders thank him for doing so.

Union chiefs who argue for dialogue, but tell the Labour leader that he must not dictate the agenda should be told firmly that this is precisely what governments are elected to do. He must be prepared to force them to square up to the truth – that free collective bargaining is a major cause of unemployment. He would not be long in office before he found it axiomatic, as did Wilson and Callaghan. (The unions know it too, but will not admit it.)

It will be hard going for Kinnock, and recent elections for top union jobs will not help him. The TGWU's successor to Ron Todd will be Bill Morris, Jamaican-born black and a welcome union breakthrough against racism. But Morris was backed by Todd and the union's left-wingers. Another pugnacious left-winger, Tony Dubbins, heads the big new print union, the Graphical, Paper and Media Union, formed from the merger of SOGAT and the NGA. USDAW, the NUM and UCATT, the tottering building workers' union, have all veered leftwards at executive level. Only in the MSF, where Roger Lyons won his campaign against hardline Communist domination to replace Ken Gill, is there any comfort for Kinnock. Even so, MSF's 1991 conference voted against 'all forms of wage restraint'.

It is extraordinary that there has been no comprehensive independent investigation of British industrial relations since the Donovan Royal Commission reported in 1968. Since then, new industries, technologies and skills, have all developed. Privatization has eroded the public sector and private monopoly has mushroomed through the giant corporations, often multinationals. The demise of manufacturing industry and of manual work has been accompanied by the burgeoning service industries and white-collar employment. Women and part-timers form an increasingly sizeable proportion of the labour force.

The unions have yet to come to grips with all this. Some still demand that Labour should repeal all the industrial relations laws put in place since 1979, including popular reforms which limit picketing, outlaw the closed shop and compel ballots for union elections and before strikes. They have yet to eschew their industrial tribalism, to produce the positive approach which might invalidate any further attempt at punitive legislation and pave the way for a more friendly government to ease them back into the mainstream of consultation, if not of decision-taking.

Tory government: union prospects

John Major is far more of a consensus politician than his abrasive predecessor, and it is possible that he would be willing to co-operate with a new-style democratic unionism. The right signals to him could pay off. Those signals would flag up the unions' belated recognition of the real needs and aspirations of working people – needs and aspirations which unions should be in business to assist, not ignore.

The touchstone must be enthusiasm for genuine and representative union democracy. The unions should embrace the laws on secret postal ballots, free from branch and workplace intimidation, as progress in the best interests of their members. They should kill off, once and for all, the irresponsible carping of those who, even now, would turn the clock back. In addition to these necessary reforms, they should consider a ten-point plan of union action for the revitalization – and indeed possibly the very survival – of the trade union movement.

(1) Unions must renounce industrial action for political ends and acknowledge that their overriding reponsibility is for the *industrial* well-being of their members.

(2) They must unequivocally reject the idea of acting outside the law and accept that the ballot box is the only way to democratic change.

(3) They must be open-minded about collective agreements, and must put the emphasis firmly on the freely negotiated right to secure a peaceful settlement, rather than on the unbridled right to strike.

(4) They must dispose of the authoritarian TUC veto on single-union, strike-free deals.

(5) They must promote more attacks on industrial apartheid by negotiating single status, eliminating the differences of employment terms and conditions between blue- and white-collar workers.

(6) They must recognize the growth of individual and employee share-ownership and profit-sharing, and should seek maximum benefits from this for employees.

(7) They must show faith in improved workers' rights, rather than rights for trade unions, and must not be scared by the consequent implication that this means more choice for workers, including the right to join or not to join a union.

(8) They must not sneer at so-called business unionism, and should seek to extend union services beyond the workplace.

(9) They must initiate more professionalism, specialization, training and education for their own full-timers and, wherever appropriate, for their members.

(10) They must work with public opinion if they are to regain any worthwhile industrial and political influence.

Unions would no doubt protest that they already encompass much of the above, and in theory they may do. However, their practical record shows that there is much work to be done.

Unions would be wise, too, to head off a long-heralded reform which a new Conservative government would be very likely to pursue – a ban on strikes in essential services. The 1981 Tory government proposal, shelved but not forgotten, was to outlaw strikes completely in certain key areas and where a strike might create a national emergency. The TUC protested long and loud at the time, but in practice it could do little against such a ban if it was introduced. It should instead take the initiative with a more modest plan of its own to make such strikes illegal unless non-binding arbitration had first been given a chance. ACAS (the arbitration and conciliation body) could draw up a model agreement to be negotiated in detail in the more vital public services. Better still, the proposal might persuade the government to revive a pigeon-holed pledge from its 1979 manifesto which promised to 'seek to conclude no-strike agreements in a few essential services'. Far from doing so, the government, worried that independent binding arbitration could prove costly, foolishly spurned the unions' offer of just such a deal at GCHQ, and thus lined up with the TUC backwoodsmen.

A government–union rethink on this is long overdue. A serious TUC initiative would be more relevant than the latest Conservative plans to add to pre-strike ballots a requirement for a seven-day cooling off period before action could be taken and to make collective agreements legally enforceable unless the parties to them jointly declare otherwise.

If the unions do march or even stumble into a new realism, it must be sustained and built upon by others. There must be a genuine attempt to produce a partnership in industry to include government, employers, unions, shareholders and employees. Nor should consumer interests be ignored. There must be renewed government intervention to stimulate competitiveness and to create a highly skilled and productive economy. Whatever the complexion of the government, ministers cannot continue to shrug off their responsibilities.

The UK's isolated intransigence over the EC social charter must end.

The Conservative government continues to oppose most of the main legislative proposals advanced by the European Commission over the shape of laws to protect individual employees. The Commission preaches the gospel of partnership in industry, whereas UK ministers cling to an approach which other Community countries have long since rejected. The TUC does now preach 'social partnership' with government and employers, though its actions continue to conflict with that aim. Its 1991 conference, for instance, voted to boycott the government's programme offering temporary jobs to long-term unemployed workers.

Industrial partnership should be underpinned by electoral reform that produces a more representative British legislature. Those trade unionists who fear that electoral reform will enshrine a virtual veto on left-of-centre government should remove their blinkers. They should recognize that such a veto negates extremism of all kinds and would stymie those espousing virulent anti-unionism.

Responsibility must be shared too, to see that the fruits of new technology are fairly and sensibly distributed and are widely enjoyed. We will all have to face up to the need for a radical restructuring of our working lives. It will mean a new kind of industrial revolution, requiring sometimes painful concessions, adjustments and compromises.

We must relate our wealth-creating capacity more closely to the manpower used. For employers, that means a more ready acceptance of innovative manpower policies, a willingness to pay for change and to pick up a larger share of the costs to the wider community of the consequent rationalization and development measures. For the unions, there will have to be a greater readiness to move from the annual wage-demand ritual to a cost-effective package that will aid both employment and productivity, and which will take on board responsibility to those without work. We are, of course, back in the area of an incomes policy, which cannot – and must not – be dodged.

Far more is needed than a mere reaffirmation of the old and increasingly meaningless commitment to full employment. If we are not to have a society based on work, if we are content to see a million or two or three of our employable population living at state expense, undignified and demoralized, then it should be a conscious and accountable decision. For our society surely believes that, apart from the elderly and those with young children, incapacitated relatives or severe disabilities, the rest of us should be given every opportunity to work for a living.

There are too many unemployed people who will never work again. Neither government, employers, nor unions, are geared to take account of the employment effects of technological change. We cannot complacently add another division to our already divided society – the prosperous few in the 'sunrise' industries versus the rest. We must avoid a society in which the micro-chip becomes a scapegoat for those who have failed to plan adequately for the nation's future and a symbol of despair for those without jobs or hope.

Trade unions should continue to play a full part in our industrial future. The extent to which they do so is largely in their own hands, but it is hard at the moment to be optimistic on their behalf. Even so, the need for a collective counter-weight to employer strength remains and will prove to be all the more important as international trade barriers crumble. Unions, like companies, will be compelled to internationalize their activities to protect their members' interests. Only a farsighted handful have begun this process.

The lesser the impact and influence of responsible trade unionism, the greater the need for it will be. Its absence will give a free run to industrial paternalism, individual contracts will increasingly be imposed to match employer demands, and across a whole range of related issues, such as training and safety, progress will be halted.

It is easily overlooked that in some of the biggest non-unionized companies, good wages and conditions for employees are the price paid to keep the unions out. Those same wages and conditions would rapidly deteriorate without unions elsewhere to set and maintain general standards.

A democratic, civilized and tolerant society requires a complexity of checks and balances, and a trade union presence is among them. It should never be forgotten that in those countries where democracy is suppressed – in much of Africa and South America, in China and until recently in Eastern Europe – free speech and free trade unionism are together in chains.

I have used the preceding pages to suggest some ways in which trade unions can revive their flagging fortunes, even if the Conservatives secure a fourth consecutive term of office, giving them the longest run of single-party government since the early nineteenth century. I shall not be thanked for my observations by the orthodox trade union top brass, but my criticisms, based on long experience, come out of my concern for better times for working people generally and for those who represent them. If partnership and co-operation could prove to be the watchwords for the nineties and beyond, it would be good for all of us.

Index